A VOICE FOR AMBASSADOR
J. CHRISTOPHER STEVENS

A VOICE FOR AMBASSADOR J. CHRISTOPHER STEVENS

By
Lydie M. Denier

Cover Design by Craig Simon

ISBN 978-0-9979366-0-5

This book is dedicated to the memory and service of Ambassador J. Christopher Stevens, Sean P. Smith, Glen A. Doherty, and Tyrone S. Woods.

CONTENTS

"No love, no friendship can cross the path of our destiny without leaving some mark on it forever"

– Francois Muria

ACKNOWLEDGMENTS

I would like to thank TUCK Magazine – without you this book would have never been published. A big thank you as well, to Annmarie Lockhart and Stan Galloway.

A special thanks to Valda Organ who has provided support, feedback, suggestions, design assistance, writing advice and editing, although we drove each other crazy at times, it was all worth it! A debt of gratitude to Gregory Hicks, as well as the people who knew Chris but who wished to remain anonymous; without you, the completion of this book could not have been possible. Heartfelt thanks, to my dearest friends, for listening and supporting me through the entire process. Thank you for your thoughts, well-wishes/prayers, phone calls, texts, and being there whenever I needed a friend. A special thanks to Terry who kept the box even though I had asked him to get rid of it! I would particularly like to thank Craig Simon for the book cover. It looks awesome! I would also like to express my appreciation to Doctor Talal Beydoun, who advised me that this is the book I should write. A big thank you to my "retired" lawyer, Robert W. Loewen, for standing beside me and staying up at night for the past three years throughout the writing of this book. Many thanks to his wife Jacinta for not interfering! Thank you to all my loved ones up there for watching over me.

Last but not least thank you to Michael, my Dane, for having the patience with me while I have taken on such an immense challenge, decreasing the amount of time we have been able to spend together.

PROLOGUE

"I'm in Benghazi this week, lurking about, my eyes ever-peeled for RPG's hurtling towards my motorcade!"

– Ambassador J. Christopher Stevens, to the U.K. Ambassador on the morning of September 11, 2012 in Benghazi, Libya.

My former fiancé, Ambassador Chris Stevens was murdered in Benghazi on September 11, 2012. During the first days after the Benghazi attack, the government was deliberately deceptive; lying to the American people about what motivated the attack, telling them that Chris was killed because a protest over an American-produced video had surged out of control, an event that occurred in Cairo, not Benghazi. The Benghazi murders occurred less than two months before a presidential election. In those days, I more or less expected politicians to lie in order to garner votes therefore I waited until the election was over for the true story to emerge. It didn't. Facts floated through the media, but there was no shape to them, no story that made sense.

This is what inspired me to search for the truth, an urge that I could not ignore. When Chris was murdered, I became obsessed with a need to know each detail about what happened in Benghazi although I was intensely aware of the gaps in the information available. Imagine a gigantic jigsaw puzzle on the floor, the random pieces scattered around in a chaos of bits of information. Each piece a vital fact provided through the media that somehow fit together with the others to complete the final picture I was attempting to form in my mind.

I cannot explain why I grieved so deeply for Chris. None of us, however, can control when and how deeply we feel a loss. When Chris was murdered, grief overwhelmed me like a huge, dark tidal wave I could not see coming. Believe me, I know how crazy this sounds, so I would not say it unless it were true: grief smacked me between the eyes almost as if I were the dead man's widow, and I know I am not that. It just felt that way, and I desperately wanted it to stop. My sorrow finally gave way to full-blown anger. Anger turned out to be the agent of change.

There would be no reason to write this book, however, if my anger had not motivated me to undertake my journey to search for the truth about Benghazi. I was persistent in pursuing that goal, speaking with people I knew from the days when Chris and I were together and others who I met along the way.

Instead of repeating what experts with a greater breadth of knowledge than I possess have already written about Benghazi, my book is about the love story that Chris and I shared when we were both young and optimistic, believing that love could overcome any obstacle. It is about the journey I have loyally and tenaciously taken in my personal search for the truth of the circumstances surrounding Chris's murder and the way in which it was reported. First love never dies. This is our story.

PART ONE

Chapter 1

Cairo, September 1994

"I am not afraid of tomorrow for I have seen yesterday
and I love today"

– William Allen White

The plane cut a tight circle toward the city of Cairo, its headlight just brushing over the thick fog. The golden city was embraced by the arms of jagged mountains, the sun reflecting off the roofs and glinting like a million diamonds. I was a 30-year-old actress who had recently found success as the character Jane in the American television series Tarzan. I had travelled to Cairo as the guest of honor to help celebrate the inauguration of a French edition of the city's paper, Al Ahram. It turned out that Tarzan, dubbed in Arabic, had become a huge hit in Egypt. A few Egyptian people significant in the movie industry would be there, including acclaimed Egyptian singer and composer George Moustaki, who was currently living in France.

Mr. Moustaki was best known for the poetic rhythm and simplicity of the romantic songs he composed and often sang. He gave France some its best-loved music by writing 300 songs for some of the most popular singers in the country such as Edith Piaf,

Dalida, and Francoise Hardy among others.

I was born in France in the province of Brittany but I hadn't yet earned the privilege of becoming an American citizen, not until 2001; therefore when I came to Egypt for the first time in 1994, I was still a citizen of France. I was however traveling on a U.S. H-1work related visa and my residence was in Los Angeles, at the time. The requirement for such a visa was that it had to be renewed every year in a foreign country. When there was time, I preferred to fly to Paris at the American embassy there. This allowed me to take the train to Brittany where I could visit my family. If I was in a hurry, a foreigner with my kind of visa was allowed to drive across the border for a renewal in Tijuana, Mexico.

Since I had been too rushed for either of those options, I called Mary Frances, the woman in charge of the inauguration in Cairo, and asked her to help me with my visa arrangements. My familiarity with the Arabic world was nil, consequently I felt slightly anxious about flying to the Middle East without this issue resolved, but I relaxed as soon as Mary said "I know someone at the American embassy. I will call him, just bring your paperwork and we will take care of it when you arrive in Cairo."

As I stepped off the plane and headed toward customs, my heart was racing with fear of the unknown. The Arab world was a scary mystery to me and I was relieved to see Mary Frances at the baggage claim. She was a woman in her mid-fifties with shoulder length brown hair that she wore loose, her mouth a thin tight red lipstick line. "Welcome to Cairo!" she said.

The ancient city of Cairo also happens to be a modern metropolis and is one of the biggest cities in the Middle East with the traffic noises to prove it. As long as you're not looking for solitude, Cairo, the City of 'The Thousand Minarets,' is an amazing place to explore Egyptian history and culture, and I saw it all. From the Pyramids of Giza, the Hanging Church, the Old City and the Opera House, just to name a few. I absorbed this place of ancient history and magic but by Friday night, after sight-seeing was over, my concern for my H-1 visa was growing as I had not yet been to the embassy. I paced my hotel room, restless and anxious.

"Have you called your friend at the embassy?" I asked Mary Frances over dinner.

"We'll go to his office this weekend." She promised.

"Is it open on weekends?"

"He'll be there." She assured me.

Late on the morning of September 11th, I walked through the doors of the American Embassy in Cairo with Mary Frances. The cream-colored walls looked beautiful from the exterior, but when I stepped inside, it felt cold, unappealing, and boring. I was dressed in jeans, closed sandals and a t-shirt that covered half of my arms, as the strict laws dictated that women were not permitted to wear tank tops, their skin always covered. I had been visiting the Egyptian Museum since 9 a.m. that morning which houses the world's most extensive collection of pharaonic antiquities. Located at Tahrir Square, it was built during the reign of Khedive Abbass Helmi II in 1897, but officially opened its doors as a museum on November 15th, 1902. It contains a total of 107 halls. The ground floor is filled with large statues while the upper floor is the resting place of mummies, their statues, jewels and Tutankhamen's treasures.

The American embassy was located in Garden City, a wealthy, residential district in Central Cairo that spans the East side of the Nile, just south of downtown and Tahrir Square. Garden City was known for its quiet, upscale and secure atmosphere, a major destination for wealthy, Western tourists. The U.S., British and Italian embassies were and still are located there as well. Despite the great political, technological, and industrial changes that occurred later in Egypt during the Arab Spring and its unsettled aftermath, Garden City managed to keep its trendy, European feel.

It had a tranquil atmosphere with its quiet, windy, tree-lined streets, beautiful gardens, and elegant, ornamental palaces and its close proximity to the American embassy made it an ideal locale. It looked more like a quaint, European village than a North African community.

The area itself was not politically active during the Egyptian Revolution. In fact, during the majority of political and technological upheaval throughout Cairo, Garden City managed to maintain its chic, first class appearance. However, due to its border with Downtown Cairo and Tahrir Square, political unrest spilled over.

Since its founding in 969 AD, Cairo has been the center of Egypt as its commerce originates there, moving through every aspect of the city. Most publishing houses, media outlets and film studios are also located within Cairo including half of its hospitals and universities.

As we approached the receptionist, a young

woman who appeared studious and no nonsense, greeted us with a polite smile.

"Hello, Ms. Frances, how are you today?"

"Hello, Helen, how are your language studies coming along?"

"I'd love them to go faster, but I'm doing fine with it. Please have a seat. I'll let Mr. Stevens know that you've arrived," she said.

We sat on a wooden bench and waited for Mary Frances' American friend, Chris.

As Mary busied herself thumbing through an innocuous magazine, my eyes followed a very tall blond blue-eyed young man in his early thirties as he left the elevator and walked through the long corridor toward the guards. I had no idea who he was, but at that moment my heart stopped. I didn't know how but that beautiful man was going to be the father of my children. He looked toward me with a resplendent smile. Later, I learned Chris and his younger brother, Tom, had been compared to the Kennedy brothers growing up and that was just how I felt when I saw him, the resemblance was uncanny.

I just kept staring, wondering how I might start a conversation. I had no idea he was Mary's 'friend' from the consulate who would help me with my visa.

There was a tethered look in Chris's eyes. The light in his face, his warming smile and his toothy wide open smile shrouded a distant but firm intelligent reconnaissance as he surveyed every inch of the room. It was almost as though he had discovered something no one else had noticed and it would require a great deal of trust before he would share it with you. Later I would come to know that when he raised his arm at a

90-degree angle, shaking his finger to make a point, there was no doubt that Chris was right about what he was saying, trust or no trust.

Oh my God! I was so affected by him that I hoped the meeting would take forever. As soon as he extended his hand to say hello, just putting my hand in his, my heart fluttered. His handshake was firm but there was a warmth too that elicited a genuine feeling of being happy to meet you.

Smiling, easygoing and friendly he said "Hello, my name is Chris Stevens."

I was speechless, unable to recall my own name! Thankfully, Mary said "This is Lydie Denier, the French actress I told you about."

Chris and I kept staring at each other, time suspended, just us alone. Chris finally broke the silence. "Let's go to my office," he said.

Before I continue further regarding our first meeting, I need to explain that this schoolgirl crush feeling that I had for Chris Stevens had never happened to me before. He simply and quite literally took my breath away.

Chris collected both of our passports, showing them to the guard for security clearance before we were permitted to make our way upstairs. While walking beside him down the hallway toward his office, I noticed the many people working there and that they all looked up to see who was with him.

When we reached his office, I noticed that he had the bare minimum: a desk, three chairs and some book shelves. He had also had several pictures hanging on the wall of an older, mother and father-type, a family portrait with a much younger Chris standing with an older couple, a younger guy who looked like his brother, and a girl. My guess was that this was his family. I noticed he wasn't wearing a wedding ring, and I hoped he wasn't married or involved with anyone. At that point, I didn't know how it would happen but I definitely wanted to see him again. I was happy to learn later that he wanted the same thing, to see me again too.

"I became enchanted with Egypt shortly after I was assigned to work here in Cairo," Chris said. "If you do nothing else, you must sail on the Nile while you're here. The view of the desert, the vegetation next to the water and the glass-like surface of the river are magnificent examples of the mingling of dualities in Egypt." Chris smiled at me.

"I've taken Lydie to the Islamic Cairo, the Mosque-Madrassa of Sultan Hassan & Al-Rifa'i, and Al Hazar Park," Mary Frances offered.

"What impressed you the most, Lydie?" Chris asked.

I felt a bit shy and flushed and at how relaxed Chris made me feel. He exuded confidence and was so charming.

"I thought the Cairo Lantern Market was particularly impressive." I said.

Chris's face exploded with excitement. "Yes, yes! He said. "The shapes, the colors, the numbers of them, what a sight!"

I smiled. He smiled. Mary Frances smiled. My heart was beating so hard and fast that I felt giddy and had to steady myself.

"Well, we'll be going on a tour together before we know it, but I do have to work," Chris said.

We laughed. "Can I see your documentation, Ms. Denier?"

When I handed it to him, our eyes met for another long moment. His gaze was powerful and it took me to a far off place, quiet and calm except for the sounds of seagulls soaring across an orange sky at sunset sliding behind purple mountains.

"Thank you." He said as he took my papers. "Give me a few minutes and I'll be right back."

It felt like it took forever for him to return and I really thought for sure there must be something wrong with my documents! Little did I know that at the same time he was trying to figure out a way to see me again. His computers were down he claimed. My heart sank and I felt terrified. I wouldn't be able to enter the States without my H-1 visa stamped on my passport. For sure now, this would require a stopover in Paris.

"Can you come back tomorrow?" Chris asked.

I couldn't. I was scheduled to go on a cruise for four days on Lake Nassar first thing in the morning as part of my contract. After the cruise, I had a flight back to the States.

The Ms. Eugenie was a five-star Egyptian cruise ship that sailed between Aswan and Abu Simbel to discover the legend of Nubia. In the 1820s, the Western world was thrilled to hear news of the rediscovery of the monuments of ancient Nubia – or 'Kush' as it is known biblically. The ruins, hundreds of miles south of Egypt in the Sudan, had been reported almost simultaneously by individual British, French, and American travelers. Their excited descriptions and glorious illustrations of temples and pyramid fields delighted scholars and reawakened interest in this mysterious African kingdom. The Nubians were black-skinned, as are the Sudanese of the same regions today. They were very striking people, tall, charcoal black skin, and their blue eyes marked them as beautiful, exotic and remarkable people.

The party for the inauguration of the newspaper Al-Ahram was that night at the same hotel I was staying, the Sheraton in the Baladin ballroom. The Ms. Eugenie would set sail next morning with me aboard. Mary Frances proposed that we rendezvous at the party to solve my visa problem.

"Why don't you keep Lydie's passport?" Mary Frances suggested. "Come to the party tonight and bring it to her." That gave him until 6 p.m. for the computers to work again.

Chapter 2

A Night to Remember

"Love consists in looking together in the same direction"

– Antoine de Saint-Exupery

After leaving the embassy, all I could think about was Chris. During lunch, I asked Mary a few questions such as how long she had known him and did his wife also work at the embassy?

Chris wasn't married (great!) and he was from San Francisco. Perfect, I thought, not too far from Los Angeles. Maybe I could see him when he visits his family.

I wore an amazing white long evening gown making me look very much like a bride. I knew he would be there; after all he was in possession of my passport!

When Chris arrived, my hands were shaking, maybe holding his a little too long when we shook hands. He completely mesmerized me. We couldn't hug since we were in a Muslim country and public affection, (particularly between a male and female) was frowned upon.

We held each other's eyes for an electric moment, and then he reached into his jacket inside pocket for my passport.

"*Voici votre passeport,* (here's your passport)" He said. Oh my God, he spoke French fluently.

"You speak French?" I asked.

"*Oui, j'ai appris la langue Francaise lorsque j'etais au Maroc.*" ("Yes, I learned the French language when I was in Morocco") he smiled.

Later that night Chris told me he had learned French and fallen in love with the people of the Middle East while teaching in Morocco for the Peace Corps from 1983-1985. Back home in San Francisco, in the early 1980's, Chris had gone to listen to a seminar at Berkeley from a couple recently retired from the Foreign Service. They explained to him that the Foreign Service was looking for people with a bit of life experience, strong language skills and that the test would be difficult. He immediately called the Foreign Service and passed the test, then called the Peace Corps to audition for a position in Morocco. Soon after, an interviewer called him to convey some good news. He had made the final cut, but they had one more question: "Do you speak French?" "Mais oui, but of course!" Chris replied. He hadn't studied French since high school, but he did take a Berlitz course. He soaked up the language like a sponge and his career in North Africa was launched. He also loved the Arabic language, which he learned while in Morocco. His gift for languages was one of the many talents that enabled him to rise quickly in the Foreign Service.

I just couldn't take my eyes off him, I was as giddy as a little kid who was biting into the chocolate coating of a Mars bar, just enough to get a piece of the single almond sitting on top with it. The anticipation, the experience, the euphoria, all I could do was look at him. I was so drawn to him that night yet we never had a moment alone together. As the guest of honor, I was being photographed from left to right. I also had to give a speech in the middle of the celebration, even saying a few words in Arabic. Then the music started and a belly dancer whirled out on the dance floor. She grabbed my hand and led me onto the floor to dance with her.

"You should dance too," I told Chris.

And he did. I laughed along with Chris, both of us caught up in the gaiety happening around us. He flashed that fabulous smile of his, beautiful white teeth, his smooth cheeks bunching up, meeting the creases at the corner of his eyes. Those eyes were so penetrating with just a pinch of mystery, perhaps teasing but always with an underlying seriousness. Unfortunately, the night was over, and I felt like we were just getting started. With all my heart I didn't want it to end. We stared at each other moon-eyed, like love-struck teenagers. I finally pressed a note with my contact information into his hand.

"Call me," I said.

His face flushed a bright red as he slid the paper in his jacket pocket. "I promise, I will." He said. "I will."

In my hotel suite, I looked out my window at the garden terrace. I longed for him, a man I barely knew. My whole body tingled, feeling as if my feet no longer touched the floor.

Chapter 3

Back in California

"To love and be loved is to feel the sun from both sides"
– David Viscott

When I returned to the States, I started working on a movie as an assistant producer. The movie 'After the Game' also known as 'The Last Hand' was distributed by Lions Gate Entertainment and I wanted to expand my knowledge of the film industry, experiencing what happens behind the scenes when you produce a film.

The story is about a man who sets out to discover how his father died after winning big in a poker game. The location for the movie was in Elko, Nevada but during filming all I could think of was Chris. He haunted my days and nights. I spoke about Chris to my best friend, Martine, who was the wardrobe designer for the film. I lost my appetite and couldn't sleep. All my waking thoughts were of nothing but him. It was impossible to concentrate. I wanted and needed to fly back home and attempt to reach Chris in Cairo.

Two weeks later when I was back in California, I called my long distance carrier to get the phone number of the American embassy in Cairo. I daydreamed for weeks how it would be if I were with Chris, not something passing in the night, but romance, love and marriage, they all fit into the equation of my fantasy. I knew I was deeply in love and I had to do something about it. I was hoping he would call me when he was in California during the holiday season, but it was months away. I just couldn't wait that long, so I called the American embassy. Yes, it was a pretty bold move, but what else could I do? I was completely smitten.

I telephoned Chris from my office, a second bedroom in my condo in Sherman Oaks, California. I was sitting at my desk sipping coffee, my stomach queasy as I waited for him to get on the line. As soon as I heard his voice on the phone, my heart started to beat faster. I had never experienced that kind of feeling before. I had only seen it in movies, but I always hoped I would someday have this kind of love. And here it was, 7600 miles away!

He was caught off guard when he answered.

"Chris, this is Lydie. You helped me with my passport."

"Wow! Hi, Lydie. What a surprise!"

Indeed, it was a surprise, even to me.

"How are you? Are you back in Los Angeles?" He asked.

"Yes, I'm back in LA., doing well. I just finished a movie. How are you?"

"I'm doing well. I'm due to leave for a meeting, so unfortunately I can't stay too long. I'd love to know more about you. Can I write to you?"

"Yes!" I said. I was so happy, we would be in contact.

"Give me your address. I will send you a card today, for sure. And I will definitely see you when I come in December, if you want to."

"Okay, I'll look forward to that." I gave him my address.

"Bye Lydie."

"Bye."

Wow... I was on cloud nine. I would definitely see Chris soon.

Later, Chris told me that as soon as he hung up the phone, he told all his colleagues: "Guess who just called me?" "The *One!*"

We promised to see each other when he was in California for the holiday season.

Not long after, I received a card with a camel on it:

Dear Lydie,

It was certainly a pleasant surprise to hear from you. I just wish we had had more of a chance to see one another while you were here. Perhaps we will (S.F., Cairo... Brittany?). In the meantime, I would enjoy hearing from you (and about you).

Chris

Chris remembered I was from Brittany. I felt special. The end of his card made me feel even more special. I paced in my office/2nd bedroom, thinking about the card as though I was lost in the jungle. In a sense, I was. It was close to 100 degrees in Sherman Oaks, where my townhouse was located. Living in the Valley was simply too hot.

Everything in my home was peach-colored including Godzilla, my teacup poodle. It had a Jungle Jane décor, a reminiscence of the "Tarzan" series. I had a wooden giraffe, a palm tree, a stuffed chimpanzee toy on the top of the pantry and a leopard carpet. The apartment was also lush with plants of all kinds, so thick that they even covered the wooden blinds. A painting of actress Hedy Lamarr I'd hung on the wall set off all of the other furnishings, because somehow, to me her sultry, beautiful look fit right into the jungle setting.

In 1986, in Hollywood, I received a beautiful gift. My first acting coach, Alan Rich, knew I was a fan of the Tarzan movies, especially those in which Johnny Weissmuller played Tarzan. For my birthday, Alan placed an original photograph of Johnny Weissmuller done by Georges Hurrell in my hands. I was so thrilled. I framed it. I hung it in my bathroom above the bathtub in a place where I could see it all the time. Prophetically, four years later I became the first French actress to play the role of Jane.

I had originally begun my career in 1985 appearing in John Denver and Ronnie Millsap's country music videos. Within eighteen months in Hollywood, I had also done twenty commercials. In 1986, actor Gary Busey saw me in a Teleflora Valentine's Day commercial. He immediately called director Steve Carver, to hire me to play his girlfriend in Bulletproof. But it wasn't until 1991 that my big break came in the Tarzan series, where I played Jane Porter. It was a new Worldvision syndicated series that lasted three years and was sold in eighty-seven countries around the world, including Egypt. Chris and I met at an important time in my career when I was busy trying to make something of that opportunity.

Chris showed a genuine interest in me. He

wanted to learn what I was about, not just superficially but deep down. This was unsettling for me, as I had never met a man like him before. And it was flattering. He was not only beautiful, his intentions were honorable. This *was* Chris. He was different, always listening, understanding what he heard and using his razor-sharp mind to try to make sense of it all in a way that would allow him to help if he could.

I could see down into the courtyard from my apartment and I had developed a habit of watching for the postman placing mail in each box, once Chris and I began corresponding regularly.

From that point forward, Chris and I began a relationship that spanned several years. Back in 1993, I saw a movie called "Shadowlands" that I absolutely adored. It's a story about C.S. Lewis, a world-renowned Christian theologian, writer and professor, who leads a passionless life until he meets a spirited poet from the U.S. who learns she has only one year to live. It starred Anthony Hopkins and Debra Winger. It was such an incredible love story. I told myself that if I had such a love, that if I were told I had a year to live, I would accept it.

Letter from Chris dated December, 1994:

Dear Lydie,

Of course, I'm counting on wishing you Merry Christmas, etc. in person, but I felt like writing anyway. You were great in "Perfect Alibi" – very convincing. You can be sure I won't be accepting any drinks – hot or cold – from you, ever!

It's been very chilly in Cairo, unusual weather. Still, I'm keeping up the tennis (my favorite sport, in case

I haven't mentioned it), trying to stay warm and in shape. See you soon, Chris.

See reverse...

Lydie,

It was a very nice surprise to get your call, and I'm glad we had the chance to speak for such a long time – we certainly didn't have that opportunity in Cairo. Glamour and all that movie star stuff aside, you are quite an intriguing person and I'm really looking forward to spending some time with you – in about 10 days, I guess! I enjoyed looking at your postcards of Brittany; they gave me a sense of your background. In that same spirit, I'm sending along a few family photos. You may even meet some of these people! Bye again,

Chris

How romantic was that? He was thinking about me, reaching out to me, wanting to touch me, wanting to be with me. It meant everything, his joking, but sensitive in nature, also complimenting me on my acting work.

Chapter 4

An Unaware Destiny

"Dance like no one is watching; Love like you'll never be hurt; Sing like no one is listening; Live like it's heaven on earth"

– William Purkey

In December, 1994, Chris sent me an article from Time Magazine about the elections in Egypt, which he reportedly had been working on, through his involvement on the streets. As I came to know him better, this level of contact with local people was a signature activity for Chris. In a 2012 New Yorker article, Robert Worth wrote:

"Chris lived to engage with ordinary people in the countries where he served."

Because such engagement, I later learned, was commonplace for Chris, it would have been interesting, except the article included the photo of a dead diplomat, Adolph Dubs, U.S. Ambassador to Afghanistan, who was assassinated in 1979. Chris reported, with typical humility, that Time Magazine's report about his effect on the Egyptian public was "overly exaggerated" and he noted, the photo was completely irrelevant to the subject at hand.

Ambassador Dubs was killed in an exchange of

gunfire during a kidnapping attempt in a Kabul hotel. Documents released from the Soviet KGB archives in the 1990's showed that the Afghan government authorized the attack despite forceful demands for peaceful negotiations by the U.S., and that the KGB adviser on scene, Sergei Batrukhin, may have recommended it, as well as the execution of one of the assailants before U.S. personnel could interrogate him. Other questions about the assassination remain unanswered.

The decision to include the photo of Ambassador Dubs in the 1994 Time Magazine article about the elections in Egypt was mostly likely human error by someone at the magazine. But to me, a person who has no logical limits on what may be discerned from coincidence, why not wonder about the connection between the mysterious murdered Ambassador Dubs and the similarly murdered Ambassador Stevens. In neither instance has the truth been told completely or at all for that matter.

Chapter 5

California: The Birth and Roots of a Diplomat

"You don't choose your family. They are God's gift to you, as you are to them."

– Desmond Tutu

C hris Stevens was a spring baby, born on April 18, 1960, the first child for Mary and Jan Stevens, a family that would later grow to include Chris's younger sister Anne and his brother Tom. A family of achievers, his father would later become Assistant Attorney General in California while his mother, a talented cellist, would perform with the Marin Symphony. It was the perfect family to nurture Chris's intellect and enthusiasm for learning, an atmosphere that encouraged the quest for knowledge that became the hallmark of his life.

The year Chris was born Elvis Presley's "Are You Lonesome Tonight" was released and Alfred Hitchcock's "Psycho" terrified moviegoers, cleaning up at the box office. The United States launched TRANSIT, its first navigation satellite and Holocaust diarist Anne Frank's home was opened to the public for the first time, personalizing the horrors of Nazi Germany through the eyes of a little girl.

A world away, the intense anti-Western revolutions of the 1960's prompted the U.S. to become more involved, often covertly, in Middle Eastern affairs. America felt obliged to defend its remaining allies, the conservative monarchies of Saudi Arabia, Jordan, Iran and the Persian Gulf emirates, with Iran, in particular, becoming a key U.S. ally.

The rapid urban expansion and development taking place in Benghazi that year were the direct result of the oil boom that forced thousands of migrant families into shanty settlements, while according to author Geoffrey Leslie Simons, "Libya's King Idris, was unable to suppress the growing political agitation among young students who were being stimulated by new ideas and foreign examples of political initiative and nationalist success."

Mohamed al-Sallabi had been among the founding members of the Muslim Brotherhood in Benghazi during the 1960's. Ali-al-Sallabi, associated with the political party "Watan," was seen as the religious leader and initiator of the effort to overthrow dictator Muammar Muhammed Abu Minyar al-Gaddafi. The developments in Libya throughout 1960, laid the groundwork for events that were to come later in Chris Stevens' life, a prophetic set of circumstances that were an echo of his future. Who could have predicted that the assassination of Muammar Gaddafi would be a forerunner of his own tragic and early death just one year later, in Benghazi on September 11, 2012.

Grass Valley, California, where Chris was born, is nestled in the Sierra Foothills just one hour from Sacramento and three hours from San Francisco. The small city was named for its spring-fed plush meadows, but its history is steeped in mining and the storied gold rush era of the 1850's.

The original white settlers came to the area from Cornwall, England to work in the tin mines as they had done in the old country, building the foundation of the city on their backs through hard work. After a disastrous collapse in the tin market, the old mines were abandoned, replaced by a far more precious metal, gold. A fever among fortune seekers was set off when gold-bearing quartz was discovered in 1850, causing prospectors to pour into the area to join the out-of-work tin miners in the search for gold. The difference between a millionaire and a pauper depended less on hard work and tenacity than it did on luck. These risk takers were apt predecessors for Chris Stevens, who was a son of this valley so rich in hope and optimism.

Although Chris's family moved away from Grass Valley, his lineage and connection always called him back as he often returned to the region to visit his grandparents, Elmer and Marguerite Stevens.

Chris loved Nevada County and he spent many happy days swimming in the wild and scenic Yuba River, with its gushing waters, deep emerald swimming holes and forested natural beauty. The family often hiked the Empire Mine State Historical Park with its rugged trails, and of course Chris jogged them. An avid runner even then, Chris especially loved the Hardrock trail as it retraced an old rail line in the woods. Chris felt a bond to Nevada County and in a way it was an intrinsic part of his identity. His respect and appreciation for the abundance of history and his ancestors' generational link to the community never faded, despite his global lifestyle that took him far from his roots.

Chris, being Chris, managed to make himself as much a part of the Piedmont community as he had a part of Nevada County, giving Piedmont an equal claim on him. In 1975, Chris's parents were divorced. This was not only a painful experience that affected him deeply, but it changed the way he lived. Both parents had always provided a loving household for their children, and the assurance since birth that both parents loved him without question made the family split less difficult for Chris. Both parents soon remarried, however, and Chris then learned to know and love two new stepparents—a tall order for a fifteen-year-old, but Chris was up to the task.

His mother married Robert Commanday. For a family that thrived on classical music, this was like marrying royalty, for Bob was the classical music critic for the San Francisco Chronicle. His father Jan, married attorney Karen Pederson who later gave birth to Chris's half-sister Hillary, now a PhD and MD in Sacramento.

Piedmont is a predominantly Caucasian, upper-middle class neighborhood that sits like an island among a multicultural, racially diverse community that spreads out into Oakland, which has many problems typical of large cities today. Sensitive to the problems of its neighbors, the community is mostly liberal politically today, but that was not always so. In the Roaring Twenties, Piedmont was known as the "City of Millionaires" because there were more millionaires per square mile than in any city in the United States.

Chris was among the most active high school

students. He participated in sports while at Piedmont High, playing football, basketball, water-polo, tennis and golf, and competed in track and cross-country. Chris especially loved tennis and played it all his life, all over the world. Running became a lifelong passion for Chris, and several among Chris's peers in the Foreign Service commented on his dedication to regular workouts, which security personnel took with him in the compound at Tripoli up until his death.

Chris also served as editor-in-chief of The Highlander, the Piedmont High newspaper, and managed to make that tough and demanding job look easy. Piedmont High also had an amazing performing arts department, and every year students put on a fall play, a holiday concert featuring both a full orchestra and *a cappella* choir, a dance concert with full jazz band, a Gilbert & Sullivan operetta, and a spring musical. Chris played saxophone in the Jazz Band, finding everything interesting and exploring his world with confidence and curiosity.

Chris wasn't transformed by the arts; they enriched him. Music and theater were always a large part of his life through his mother's involvement with music and his stepfather's work as a conductor and music critic. Chris had a flair for the dramatic too. His brother Tom and his sister Anne recall Chris's early antics when he loved to run around pretending he was a superhero or a spy. The arts allowed Chris to cultivate and hone skills using instincts he already possessed.

Both jazz and diplomacy involve a solid structure with natural progressions and require a complete command of the notes you're supposed to play, but they also involve improvisation, requiring the players to listen to the sounds of other instruments, respect the improvisation of others, giving them the time to develop their own licks so that the sounds of the performers can meld together.

Jazz is, famously, also about the notes you don't play and jazz lover Chris also knew this power of silence. Colleagues in the Foreign Service remarked on Chris's talent for sitting quietly sipping coffee during a conversation or negotiation waiting for the information he needed. Like jazz, diplomacy is more art than science, and Chris was an accomplished artist.

During his junior year at Piedmont High, Chris traveled to Spain as an AFS Intercultural Program exchange student, an experience that sparked his interest in foreign travel and learning languages, as well as satisfying his lust for adventure. A seed had been planted that would grow and blossom.

Chris graduated from Piedmont High in 1978 and in his high school yearbook he quoted essayist Logan Pearsall Smith:

"What a bore it is, waking up in the morning always the same person. I wish I were unflinching and empathic, and had big, bushy eyebrows and a message for the age."

So where are Chris's roots? I have to say both places. He had the work ethic, common sense and nerve of the risk takers found in the heritage of Grass Valley, but he developed the sophistication and training needed for diplomacy while living in Piedmont. Together, they gave the world a well-rounded and extraordinary man.

Chapter 6

Brittany: The Birth and Roots of an Actress

"Within ourselves, there are voices that provide us with all the answers that we need to heal our deepest wounds, to transcend our limitations, to overcome our obstacles or challenges, and to see where our soul is longing to go."

– Debbie Ford

I was born, on April 15th 1964 in Trignac, a little village in the countryside in South Brittany, France. The setting was straight out of a Jane Eyre novel and it shaped my entire life. A small house, white with yellow shutters, built in the middle of the woods, garnished the landscape. It was one of those cabins built to house fishermen during the long fishing seasons, well hidden in the middle of nowhere. It was so peaceful and quiet with just the sounds of frogs and crickets blending together as the sun set down. A delicious breeze gently caressed my face during summertime and the sound of branches scratching against the windows, during wintertime, just like in a horror movie, sharpened my senses.

In 1964, President Lyndon Johnson declared a

war on poverty that helped pave the way for Medicare and Medicaid while the Beatles stormed America. Sidney Poitier became the first African-American to win an Oscar for best actor; Nelson Mandela was sentenced to life in prison in South Africa; the Palestinian Liberation Organization was established; Congress passed the Gulf of Tonkin Resolution; the U.S. became fully involved in the Vietnam War; Egypt ended the stage of siege and Martin Luther King Jr. was awarded the Nobel Peace Prize.

Hollywood had such an impact on my life as a child. Growing up in the countryside of Brittany, France, there were always two American movies every Wednesday night and Sunday afternoons. They weren't new releases; they were always from the Hollywood era of the thirties and forties. So I was not surprised in 1989, when the casting director for General Hospital, Marvin Page, told the producers he had a young Hedy Lamarr sitting in his office. I had grown up watching Hedy Lamarr films and in many ways these movies were my first acting class.

I was cast to play the role of Yasmine Bernoudi in General Hospital and as a femme fatale; my character had three lovers on the show, one for money, one for status, and one for love. She was very much like Joan Collins' character on Dynasty. I was working five days a week. My days started early every morning at 7am, often ending so that I got back home after 6pm, staying up late to learn my lines for the next day. The idea of having time for a committed relationship escaped me.

When my contract expired, from this point forward, my life was going full blast. I was going from one job to another, from one location to another, from one photo shoot to another and from one commercial to another.

Acting became my only focus. I took more acting lessons with Ivana Chubbuck in Hollywood, one of the most sought after acting coaches and teachers in North America. I had previously attended the "Lee Strasberg Theater" also in Hollywood. Aspiring actors are dreamers. My dream was to become a professional actor. I wanted to be successful. I had dreamt of it so many times. I was determined to succeed. A relationship would just get in the way. It would happen when it was supposed to happen. And I most definitely didn't want to be with someone in the business.

Ivana has a gift for reading people; she discerns the darkest secrets in unwitting detail and uses that knowledge to challenge them to use these details in the roles they play. Ivana is an actor whisperer. She will do anything she needs to do to bring out the best in her students and that usually makes her aggressive, physical and vulgar. If you are her student, you had better be ready to take a lot of abuse, tell the truth about yourself and work hard all the time, or you will be gone. In Ivana's class, there is no time for victims and whiners. Every actor must know what the character's objective is in order to win someone's love, respect, or sympathy. Every actor must be ruthless about achieving that objective. "And as in the scene", teaches Ivana, "so in life." I believed every word Ivana taught me. I practiced it in every audition and every role I won.

And now, love was staring me in the face. Ivana taught me nothing about love and all her lessons made no sense when it came to Chris. I knew this man was going to change everything for me because I was prepared to do anything for him.

When I was growing up, my favorite subject at school was history, especially Egypt, its mummies and Tutankhamen. This, as other parallels between Chris and I, surfaced here in my thinking. Egypt and Chris, Egypt and me; Fate possibly but who could say?

I loved being at school. I was the happiest there. I was a very good student, always hungry to learn more. My Dad told me that starting at the age of five, I used to read lots of books about far away countries. I craved to be a good student, one of the best. And I had been just that. In my teenage years, my dream was to be a reporter/journalist, covering wars. But studies were too expensive and my parents couldn't afford it.

At age seven, my school celebrated "La Galette des Rois". It is a way for French people to celebrate the Epiphany, the arrival of the Three Wise Men. Every year, on January 6th, people gather to find the kings. The traditional galette is cut in a very specific number of slices: One slice for each person sitting at the table plus one. The extra slice is symbolic for the first poor person passing by. A lucky charm, la feve, is hidden in the galette. The person that gets the slice with the lucky charm becomes "the king" or "the queen" for the day and you get to choose your king or queen.

I got the lucky charm and one of my cousins, Gilbert, got a lucky charm too. He picked a girl to be his queen. And I picked the boy I was secretly in love with, Jean-Marc, a blond, blue-eyed boy, a Brad Pitt look-alike.

As soon as I got the lucky charm, I grabbed him

and held him tight. He couldn't escape! Now as a queen, he was mine! Parents laughed out loud. It looked so funny. A few pictures were taken and Jean-Marc had his eyes wide open while my own face exploded in excitement.

As a little girl growing up in Brittany, I held all Americans in the highest esteem. Even in the 1970's reminders were everywhere of those American heroes who had come to liberate France from the German invaders. There were not only memorials where the names of men long dead were carved and wreaths laid, but also the bunkers and tank entrapments where the brave American men fought and died to free Europe from the horrors of World War II.

Chris epitomized my belief that all Americans were the same as those brave soldiers at Normandy. He was like those men who set out to help, not to conquer, heedless of the risk to their own safety. During that brief encounter on the dance floor, Chris made me feel safe and secure. On my flight back to Los Angeles from Cairo, I knew in my heart that I had found my American hero and just had to figure out a way to bridge the 7,576 miles between us so I could see him again.

Chapter 7

The Holiday Season

"It is better to look ahead and prepare than to look back and regret"

– Jackie Joyner-Kersee

T he holiday season was soon upon us and Chris arrived in San Francisco. Within a few days I was on a plane to see him. He had two weeks' vacation, so I flew there to be with him for three days. It was a heavenly time. He picked me up at the airport, waiting for me at the gate. We hugged and his cologne, subtle but nearly overpowering because he was the one wearing it, intoxicated my senses. When I leaned against his chest I could feel his beating heart next to me. I could hear him breathing, a sound like whispering without words. We lingered for a moment, which felt like an eternity to me and a feeling I had been searching for all my life surfaced: Safety, Security and love. I was almost afraid it was going to dash away, disappearing forever. The blue of his eyes was even more hypnotic than I remembered.

We stayed in the Hotel Juliana on Bush Street, a boutique style hotel only six blocks from the ultra-modern Moscone Convention Center and Buena Gardens. While it retains a historic 1903 flavor, its distinctly European-style lobby is elegant, yet intimate, centering on a cozy fireplace. We checked in, and like two high school students we scrambled up to the bedroom in a hurry.

Inside the cozy king size bedroom, we threw our bags on the floor. Chris approached me, took my face in his hands and kissed me and what a kiss it was, such passion! His kisses left me stunned, reeling and longing to fill the emptiness inside I had never before acknowledged. My whole body tingled. More kisses and my knees weakened. I swear I felt I went to heaven; it was such a rush of emotion! I could feel my face flush as I walked to the bed.

Chris was bold, blatantly, sensually evocative. His touch was exquisite. His hands moved on me so slowly, so languidly. Yet there was heat in every caress. A blatant sensuality burned through my veins. Passion and desire were twin flames. My senses reeled. I absorbed the sensations. His touch warmed me, excited me. It made me glow. His eyes were like two blue hypnotic pools.

I reacted to each sensual tactile taunt, each caress and each teasing glide. His lips played on mine. His fingers played on my skin. Desire, illicit pleasure, jolted through my spine. I waited, tight with expectation and sensual anticipation. He tantalized my senses. He played deliberately, focused on my grasp, attuned to every quiver, every restless shift. He stripped away every last vestige of modesty with a ruthless gentle touch until I was panting, wanting, aching and so desperate for more.

The next morning we had breakfast in, then lunch at a café in downtown San Francisco. We went for walks on Stinson beach, later dining in the theater district. It was cozy and very romantic, as if we were on our honeymoon.

A photo shoot I had planned interrupted our otherwise romantic time together. I had recently purchased the rights to the Hedy Lamarr story and a photographer was going to film me as Hedy Lamarr taken with the Bolex, a favorite of independent filmmakers and specialist cinematographers in the 1930s, mainly because it has great features such as single frame and, in some models, auto fades in and out. Chris popped in that afternoon to see me with his sister, Anne.

Chapter 8

Meeting Chris's Family

"Love is just a word until someone special gives it
a meaning."

– Unknown

C hris asked me to stay longer because he wanted
me to meet his mother and stepfather. The
Juliana was booked with no spare rooms
available, so Chris suggested we would spend the night
at his parents.

Chris's mother Mary was very hospitable and
showered her attention on Chris. Chris's step father
Bob, a former theater and music critic, was a down-to-
earth man who made me feel comfortable and at home.
His family shared lots of hugs together. Both Chris's
father's and his mother's families came together for the
holidays. I was amazed.

My family was quite different, the opposite
actually. The missing story really starts before I was
born, when my mother and father met and quickly
married. My dad, an emotionally strong man with jet
black hair and a steel look in his deep green eyes put a
sparkle in every woman's eyes. He loved the ocean more
than the fish themselves.

My mother was a beautiful, impracticable

creature, a model type with deep blue eyes and long wavy blondish hair. She always dreamed of being someone from the high class society but worked as a waitress in a local bar "La Bretonne".

On July 20th, 1963, my parents said, "I do!" After the ceremony, my mother tried to commit suicide in the Ile & Vilaine River. Nine months later, I was born into a world of lies and illusions. My eyes as a child wandered sadly without knowing where I fit in the world of adults.

My parents worked hard to put a roof over our heads. My dad's job took him to different towns every day to sell meats to businesses, companies, schools, different outside markets and private buyers but my parent's marriage was chaotic, to say the least. And on November 2nd, 1976, my mom closed the book on dad and they haven't spoken since.

Chris's family couldn't have been more different from mine. For the most part, although exhibiting high intellect as a family, they were pragmatic people who chatted and joked about the weather, politics, sports and pop culture.

"Were the Dallas Cowboys really going to win the Super Bowl?" "What about Tonya Harding having some men including her husband breaking Nancy Kerrigan's kneecap?"

There were also serious-minded discussions about Kurt Cobain's suicide, serial killer Jeffrey Dahmer, John Candy's unexpected death and Richard Nixon's passing. Family members also openly discussed what was going on in their lives. They were simply divorced parents, very civilized with each other, who stayed friends and spent holidays together.

Chris was the source of humor in his family, always crossing over to someone else, getting in their shoes, and saying or doing something that made them laugh. He loved making people laugh. His sister, Anne, talked about how clever and witty Chris was and how he made them smile. He was very mischievous.

He told her once how he set her bassinet on fire, led her off a hiking trail, and nicknamed her 'Chubs'. His brother Tom once told the story of how Chris set the basement on fire with a magnifying glass. He also had the power of subtle persuasion, and once he Talked Tom into stripping, donning a ski mask, and running through the neighbor's house while they were watching television.

Tom never saw Chris ever yell at or hit anyone. Chris always thought clothes made the man but he was a very humble guy. He never sought to get credit. He just cared about other people. He stayed positive. He did it right. He was calm and steady. When he shook hands to say goodbye, he always said, "I'll see you next time."

The following day after our visit, Chris and I drove to Sacramento where his dad, Jan, and stepmom, Karen, lived with their daughter Hillary. We spent the night with them. The next day after that, all of us drove to Lake Tahoe to ski. His mom, stepfather, sister Anne and brother Thomas, met us there. Chris tried to put me on skis and it was a disaster. I had never skied before.

During the winter, the Stevens family skied at Donner summit, a critical route across the Sierra Nevada Mountains for centuries. Along with his siblings, Chris learned to ski at an early age, and as with so many things Chris chose to do, he was a natural. Chris was very competitive, and it showed in everything he did as he was never the type to take the easy way out. Although both sets of parents, his siblings, Tom, Anne and Hillary were avid skiers, at times it was challenging to keep up with the focused athlete they watched Chris become, as he grew up on the ski slopes.

Chris encouraged me to try cross-country skiing, telling me I could do it because I was athletic. Mary and Karen joined us and off we went while his three other siblings, Bob and his father went skiing. Well, I wasn't very good at it! But Chris, optimist that he was, said: "With practice, you will get better and we will have plenty of occasions to ski again."

My mind and heart were whirling about Chris. Meeting his family and participating in activities with them began to leave an indelible impression on me. Chris was looking at me beyond that of a brief romantic interlude.

Chris always spent the holiday season with his family. He never missed one no matter where he was in the world. In contrast, my mother never wanted to celebrate Christmas Eve. And on Christmas Day, she always wanted to go to her mother's house, never with her in-laws. For my baby sister's first Christmas, Santa Claus brought a rocking pony. Why did Santa Claus forget to bring me one too? I got up from my bed very early that Christmas Day and as I poked through the wrapping paper I could see the pony's ears. I was sad as I saw nothing I had wished for under the tree. Instead I got a book on Geronimo and two oranges. As soon as my parents turned their backs, I jumped on the pony. It was fun. But my mother heard the ding-dong sound from its collar, ran back into the living area, and ordered me to get off that pony. It wasn't mine. It was for my baby sister!

The following Christmas was different, my grandmother, Nana, gave me a child piano that I cherished; I loved it, practiced and became a proficient player. I still have it.

Chapter 9

Love Is

"I am who I am today because of the choices I made yesterday"

– Eleanor Roosevelt

C hris flew to Los Angeles to spend New Year's Eve with me on the last day of 1994. I picked him up at LAX airport. His gaze touched me everywhere, even as he stared into my eyes, his own filled with both desire and heat. When his lips touched mine my lips quivered under his. Our breath mingled, our lips separated slightly. His touch made me glow. Then my lips met his again, but this time, soft, generous, and hesitant. The urge to devour him was strong. My breasts had swollen.

We had booked three nights at the Malibu Beach Inn, a hotel painted extremely pink. As soon as we were in our room, I felt the desire burning inside him with each step he took towards me. His hand grasped my arm and pulled me back up against his chest. His warm breath caressed the bare skin of my shoulders. My heart skipped a beat as my breasts smashed into his chest. The thick, moist air stirred our bodies hot and sweaty. He slipped one of his hands beneath my T-shirt. His fingers fanned across my stomach. I slowly swirled around. I looked him into his eyes, holding his gaze. My eyes were as intense as his. His pulse quickened and began to race. I wrapped my arms around his neck. His hands on my body warmed me, excited me.

When we were not making love, we took long walks on the beach, enjoyed romantic dinners by candlelight and rode bicycles along the beautiful bike paths. Chris asked me detailed questions about my work. He was incapable of superficial inquiry; he drilled down on every subject from becoming an actress to preparing for a role. Most importantly he wanted to know whether I liked it and why. Unlike most men, Chris genuinely cared about my happiness, not only as it related to him but in all respects. When we did spend time in the room, he wrote in his journal, which he carried with him everywhere. I like to read and took the opportunity to catch up on it. It was easy to be in the same room, so natural to be together. The intimacy we shared during that time is imprinted on my mind and heart. Parting was difficult but both of us had lives separate from each other in miles and in vocations.

Letter from Chris dated January 8, 1995, written in the morning:

Dear Lydie,

As long as I live, I'll never forget the four wonderful days we had together in Malibu. It went by so quickly. I remember you standing, smiling, waiting to meet me when I arrived, walking off with you snugly under my arm; and I remember our long goodbye that rainy miserable day (made doubly miserable because our little paradise was ending and I had to fly away in a storm!).

What happened in between? Speaking for myself, I found that it is very easy to be with you. Whether we were out or in, on a mountain or riding a bike down the beach, I felt relaxed and happy. My favorite moments were our mornings on the trail followed by brunch at Saddle Peak, our late afternoon walk along the beach and sipping Chianti by the fire learning about your work (I learned so much! It's all new to me!), and watching old movies with you, your head tucked under my arm (or my head resting on your shoulder as I began to doze off into sweet oblivion...).

I also discovered, or rather confirmed, that I am extremely attracted to you. Could you tell? I could easily hold you for hours, kissing, caressing you.

What I'm slowly discovering and appreciating more and more are the qualities of your character and personality that, because of the way you are, I didn't immediately see. Especially your love and commitment, and the mature and clear-eyed way you view a relationship as something that doesn't just happen by itself but that requires attention, energy, commitment, and trust. You are so right. Lydie, you are always in my thoughts and in my heart.

I love you,
Chris

In the envelope was another letter written on the same day, but in the evening after he had come home from a dinner at his best friend Taieb's house. Taieb was the son of the Tunisian Ambassador in Cairo.

Dear Lydie,

It's cold and grey here in Cairo, cold enough to wear my huge Turkish leather coat, which, after you told me it looked good on me, I've suddenly begun to like it much more! I put it on this evening (after talking with you) and walked to Taieb's house to have dinner with him and his father who, as I told you, is the Tunisian Ambassador to Egypt.

The meal was delicious, prepared by their Tunisian cook, and since Taieb's father doesn't speak English or the Egyptian dialect in Arabic, we spoke in French. We had a very interesting conversation about the situation in Algeria, and about the relationship between the West and Islamic countries in general. He thinks France's policy of supporting the Algerian government's crackdown on the Islamists is preferable to the U.S. policy of trying to negotiate with them. He thinks that if the extremists are allowed to take control, hundreds of thousands of Algerians will flee to France, and an extremist Algerian government will export its extremist policies to neighboring countries, like Tunisia.

I agree with him, that these are the likely results of an extremist Islamic government taking control, but are the current brutal crackdown the best way to prevent the extremists from taking power? Or is it simply making them and their friends and relatives, angrier? Extremists like those in Algeria are on the rise throughout the Near East, challenging their governments and expressing hatred for the West. How to best handle these difficult people is one of the most interesting questions facing us in the State Department.

But I didn't sit with him with the idea of writing to you about foreign policy! After dinner, Taieb and I sat in the living-room talking about you, among other things. He thinks ours is a great story, and he hopes it has a happy ending. And so do I, although you might not think it; I know I'm not the most demonstrative person in the world. Like my father, I have always been a little reserved when it comes to expressing my feelings. But I realize that it is important to share one's feelings, and I've gotten better over the years, especially since Bob entered our lives, who is probably the most demonstrative person in the world, and since realizing that my mother and father broke up 18 years ago because my mother felt that she couldn't talk to him about their relationship, or, more accurately, that he wouldn't talk to her. So, I'm very sensitive to this shortcoming of mine, and hope that if you ever feel that I am shutting you out or hiding something from you, you might be a little patient with me and help me talk to you. It will be worth the effort, I can assure you. But as I told Taieb tonight (Taieb is like Martine; he is my closest "confidant"), there is no one better. And I mean that.

If you were just beautiful, I might be attracted to you but I wouldn't be as serious as I am about you. There are so many more things about you that I admire – your talent, your independence, your drive and self-discipline, your great capacity for affection, your loyalty (I have a strong feeling that I can trust you), and your fearlessness of flying!

Lydie, I think we have great potential and I am committing myself to you and to us. Are you with me?

Love,
Chris.

The last line in the letter, "I think we have great

potential and I am committing myself to you and to us. Are you with me?" made my heart jump.

In the envelope was another letter dated January 10th, 1995:

Hi again,

I wanted to add another note before I send this off to you in Las Vegas. How is it going? Working hard?

I'm still recovering from jet lag. Last 2 days I've been going home from work at 5 and immediately falling asleep for 4 hours, waking up at 9 for dinner! Then I have a hard time getting back to sleep. Yesterday I was supposed to meet some friends to see "Lion King" but slept through the rendezvous, very embarrassing.

Our new boss, the consul general, is very friendly and a great talker. He's Asian and used to be an English professor at Ohio State. He's looking forward to meeting you!

Guess who I bumped into today on the way to the cafeteria? Mary Frances! She's everywhere! She's working on her marathon and plans to stay till the end of the month. I did not mention you or our vacation in California.

Well, Sweetheart, I continue to miss you and look forward to hearing your voice.

Love,
Chris

Chapter 10

Vodka, Peanuts and Me

"If you aren't going to go all the way, why go at all?"

– Joe Namath

In mid-January 1995, after I finished filming the movie 'To the Limit' in Las Vegas with Anna Nicole Smith, Chris and I missed each other so much that I flew to Cairo to spend one week with him.

I was on TWA Flight 800 with a stop in New York, a stop in Paris and final stop in Cairo. I took the same flight each time I flew to Cairo to see Chris. In July 1996, TWA Flight 800 crashed when the plane, headed for Paris, exploded and fell into the Atlantic Ocean shortly after takeoff from John F. Kennedy International Airport. All 230 people aboard died. Some witnesses saw a streak of light and a fireball prior to the explosion and this unleashed a bevy of speculations that terrorists had struck the plane with a rocket. The NTSB said the explosion resulted from fumes in an empty fuel tank. Either way, it didn't miss me by much.

When I met Chris, I knew nothing about politics and could care even less. Chris, however, was intensely interested in everything political. I told him I would like to meet President Clinton because I thought he was handsome, which made him laugh, but he said I should pay attention to politics because policy matters. As a diplomat, it was his job to serve under any president the people elect, Democrats or Republicans, so he could not choose sides publicly, but some policies work better than others in foreign affairs, he said, and his job was made easier when the right policies are followed. Because Chris was always evenhanded in the way he saw things, this is how I received my education in politics and foreign policy. Unlike the polarized arguments we hear today, Chris was brilliant at presenting the positions of all sides in its best light and then explaining the flaws in those arguments too. Soon I was expressing my own opinions on politics and other subjects as I found myself reading the newspaper more thoroughly to keep up.

Chris was a natural teacher, and he certainly provided me with many new interests that I still carry to this day. But looking back, perhaps the love I felt for him grew even more because of the respect he showed in talking to me as an equal about his favorite subjects, and his eyes would shine with love when I argued back and tried my best to give it back to him when we disagreed.

When Mary Frances, the organizer of my first appearance in Cairo who had introduced me to Chris, knew I was back in Cairo, she invited me once again to be a guest of honor, this time in the Miss Egyptian Beauty Pageant.

Chris and I had an amazing time together. I even had a pet name for him very early on in our relationship, "my skinny chicken". Chris was and always had been a very skinny guy with very long and skinny white legs. I used to compare him, with love, to a skinny chicken. This pet name always stayed with him. But in front of others, I called him my "Habibi", which means "my love" in Arabic.

Every night, when he came back from work, he loved having a little glass of vodka and some peanuts, much like his father. He was also a creature of habit and every morning, Chris dutifully polished his shoes before he went to work. Otherwise, flip-flops and sandals were the "shoes" of the day for him.

Vodka and peanuts was all that Chris had in his kitchen cupboard, and of course, he had me as well. And it is with vodka and peanuts that his family commemorated the first anniversary of his death on the beach, September 11, 2013.

Chapter 11

Valentine's Weekend

"Dream as if you'll live forever, live as if you'll die today"

– James Dean

During Valentine's Day weekend we escaped the craziness of Cairo for two days. Because we both loved to hike, Chris was anxious to show me the beauty of Mount Moses, which Americans know better as Mount Sinai, a 7,497-foot mountain with 3,750 steps hewn out of stone by monks of St. Catherine's Monastery. When we arrived at the top of the mountain, a visitor took a picture of us with my camera. We used this beautiful photo in the announcement of our engagement.

The next stop on Chris's guided tour was Saint Catherine's Monastery, just to the north of the mountain where monks had carved the steps. Saint Catherine's monastery, commonly known as Santa Katarina, lies on the Sinai Peninsula, at the mouth of a gorge at the foot of Mount Sinai, in the city of St. Catherine in Egypt's South Sinai Governorate. Chris explained to me that the monastery is Orthodox and is a UNESCO World Heritage Site, exactly like the Mont-Saint-Michel in France. One of the oldest monasteries in the world, it was built between 548 and 565. Not far away, there's a small town with hotels and swimming pools called Saint Catherine City.

We stayed for two nights in one of the hotels, the Daniela Village Sainte Catherine.

Chris knew so much about everything. When he didn't know a place, he would research everything about it, very much like me. Because I started my career at a young age, I never attended college therefore I learned to teach myself through reading and research. Travelling and discovering places together brought us closer to each other. We shared a passion for adventure.

Chris shared the history: "Let me tell you about Catherine of Alexandria," his eyes lit up. "She was a Christian martyr, sentenced to death on the wheel, a torture device used for capital punishment in the middle Ages and early modern times for public execution by bludgeoning to death. It looked like a large wooden wagon wheel with numerous radial spokes. When the wheel failed to kill her, she was beheaded. According to tradition, angels took her remains to Mount Sinai. Around the year 800, monks from the Sinai Monastery found her remains." I was mesmerized listening to all the great stories. I was so happy to be here, with him.

On the drive back, Chris told me about another monastery, Saint Anthony: "It's hidden deep in the Red Sea Mountains. Monks still lived there."

"Let's go visit it!" I said with excitement, not wanting our day to end.

"It's getting late. If we want to be back in Cairo before nightfall, we should keep driving. We'll go another time," he said.

But I wanted to know more. I was thirsty to learn more about Egypt, its culture, and its tradition, and what better teacher than Chris.

"I want to see it. Let's go now!" I insisted.

"Then let's go! I have never been there. It is a place we can discover together." He smiled.

The Monastery of Saint Anthony is a Coptic Orthodox. It stands in an oasis in the Eastern Desert of Egypt, in the southern part of the Suez Governorate. Hidden deep in the Red Sea Mountains, it is located 334 km (208 miles) southeast of Cairo.

Saint Anthony was a Christian saint who was born to a wealthy family in Lower Egypt around 251 A. D. At the age of 34, Anthony donated to the poor all of his property and worldly possessions; he ventured into the Eastern Desert to seek a life of humility, solitude, and spiritual reflection. He made his abode in a small cave where he devoutly practiced an ascetic life. Although St. Anthony was not the first monk, he attracted many followers and disciples, and is one of the fathers of modern Christian monasticism.

The drive was beautiful with amazing scenery. I looked toward Chris and he seemed lost.

"What's wrong?" I asked.

"The monastery should be coming soon. We should see a small road to turn left into, and that will take us directly at its foot." He answered.

His answer wasn't exactly responsive and certainly not what I was accustomed to, hmm. We kept driving, and driving.

"Maybe I missed the turn. It's going to get dark soon. I think we should just keep driving back home!" Chris said.

I thought, "No way!" Up to that point in our relationship, I had been treating Chris like a Greek God, and he was actually living up to the role with his greatest everything. But now I thought, "He is just lost and won't admit it. No way is he going to keep me from seeing that monastery!" I grabbed the map from inside the glove compartment. "Okay, let's see. What did you say the name of the place was?"

"You're a very persistent woman. I like that." He said. "You remind me of my mother. When she wants something, she doesn't let go! I like that."

A lot changed at that point. Chris admitted later he had been playing his own note to try to meet the high expectations I had of him and I, in turn was not willing to acknowledge that Chris was just a man—a pretty terrific man—but a man with flaws like not admitting when he was lost. I loved this man with man-flaws so much more. A few months later, Chris told me that was the day he knew he wanted to marry me. And we did find the monastery!

After spending a couple of hours visiting with the monks, we were finally driving back to Cairo. It was really late, later than we should have been on the road. It was very dark. And the road seemed longer than it took us on the way to Mount Sinai. At that point, I looked over at Chris, who was driving.

"Are you lost?" I asked.

Chris kept his eyes sharply on the road.

"No, I'm not." He said.

"Here we go again," I thought.

"Are you sure?"

"Of course I'm sure."

"I think we're going around the block. We're

definitely driving around the block. We're driving in circles."

The dash lights in the car cast enough light on Chris's face and I noticed his forehead wrinkle.

"Well, what made you say that?" He asked.

"It's the camel." I said. "We keep seeing the same camel we saw earlier. I think we're going around the mountain. I think we're lost."

"It's a camel. Camels all look alike."

"It's the same camel. We are lost." Men will admit to committing murder before they will admit they're lost.

Chris eventually found a marker that helped us get back to Zamalek. And that reminded me of another story. Throughout his travels, Chris always wrote wonderful letters to friends, family and loved ones, about his experiences. Once he told me he went out for a run near the village where he was staying in Morocco.

Some locals ran alongside him and asked, "Where is it? "Where did it go?"

"Where is what?" asked Chris.

"Your donkey, where did it go?" asked one of the locals.

"I don't have a donkey!"

"Then, why are you running?"

"For exercise."

"Exercise? If you want some exercise why don't you come work in my orchard, you crazy American!"

Chapter 12

The Proposal

"I promised to stand by you, to hold you up when you're
about to fall, and to always keep you safe. I never
believed there was a girl out there for me, until I met
you. You changed everything. And I never want to live
without you. I love you more than I ever
thought possible."

– J. Sterling

Two days later, February 14th, 1995, was
Valentine's Day, our first together. Chris took me
to the Windows on the World restaurant on the
36th floor of the Ramses Hilton hotel overlooking the
Nile River. The stunning panoramic views over the Nile
and Pyramids in this stylish restaurant offered
international cuisine, cocktails and evening
entertainment in the romantic low lighting and
contemporary décor of the showcase bar.

At that time, February 1995, a more famous
version of Windows on the World offered fine dining in
Manhattan. Many disappointed tourists learned that
reservations made far in advance were an absolute
requirement if you were visiting New York City and
wished to enjoy the unmatched view from the 107th
floor of the World Trade Center. Back in Cairo we gave

no thought to other restaurants, other cities, or even other people. And we were completely oblivious to the horrible future six and a half years away when a handful of terrorists would carry out the planned murder of thousands of innocents, including the seventy nine employees working at Windows on the World restaurant who died that day without knowing why. But for that one blissful Valentine's Day at Windows on the World in Cairo there was only us, Chris and me.

That day, Chris went on his usual run right after work. But when he returned, he had a focus that penetrated me.

"Are you okay?"

"I have to see Taieb at the Tunisian Ambassador's house." He said while changing his clothes.

"Why?"

"I'll tell you when I get back." He kissed me on the lips.

I fussed about not really doing anything that constructive. I washed and fixed my hair and started reading a book, of which I have little memory. Just like that, Chris was back.

We were seated by the window. What a magnificent view! But it was impossible to relax because Chris was fidgeting in his chair, not at all his normal self. He reached out his hand, palm up on the table, and I reached too, allowing him to caress mine. His hand, usually so masculine and sure, was wet and slightly clammy. At that moment I knew. He is going to propose, I thought.

"Yes!" I said, too loud, I am sure. I could not

believe I had blurted the answer before he even asked the question.

"Yes, what?"

"Yes, I will marry you. Isn't that what you were trying to ask me?"

Chris began to laugh. "Yes it was. How did you know?"

I was laughing too mostly because I was giddy with happiness but also covering my own embarrassment. "Ok. Let's start over." He said. "Pretend I have not said anything."

By this time, the few people in the restaurant were staring at us with big smiles.

"Lydie Denier, will you be my wife?"

"Yes, Chris Stevens, I will."

Then he leaned across the table and kissed me. And just like that, we were engaged.

Chris explained that he was having a ring specially made by a jeweler but that it was not ready yet. I told him, I did not need a ring. I only needed him.

When we returned to his apartment, we were like two teenagers, kissing and petting. I wanted to make love, but Chris wanted to call his mother to give her the good news. Mary and Bob, his stepfather, both got on the line before he told them we were engaged. There was a long silence from the California end of the line. Finally, Bob said, "I knew it! I knew it!" Mary, the cellist, who he loved more than anyone, was silent.

Naturally, I was worried. I had felt the resistance from Mary when I visited Chris's family. Chris was close with his family, especially his mother; it was one of the things I loved best about him. Would his love for me survive if his family, especially his mother, disapproved?

The more I thought about it, the more I became angry at the idea of all of it. Why the hell should his family disapprove of me? For loving their son like he was my last breath? There's nothing better than having a man like Chris who has shaken you inside and out, knows who you really are, acknowledges your differences, and loves you completely. They had met me. By their standards, I am not educated because I pursued an acting career instead of college, but I am pretty sure they recognized that I am not stupid. Chris and I both recognized the differences between us. I wanted to explain to Mary that those differences are not disqualifying; Chris and I had embraced them and viewed them as strengths in our relationship. Chris was eager to teach me about his world, and I was hungry to learn.

We were brought up differently, and I did not have all the advantages that Chris did. But what I had in Brittany was not useless and I had learned things from that life. Together, Chris and I planned to blend the best from both of our worlds. Chris saw great potential in me, he said, and I always had confidence in myself. Most importantly, Chris treated me with respect. The differences that others believed were huge for Chris were only superficial because at our core we were the same. I loved him for that.

Later that night, after dinner, he explained that when he had disappeared before we went out, he had gone to see Taieb. He asked his confidant a question: "I'm thinking about asking Lydie to marry me. What do you think?"

Taieb smiled. "Go for it!"

I have viewed Taieb as a friend and ally ever since. He was the first to call me when Chris died; knowing before I did how much Chris's death would affect me.

I returned home a few days later.

Letter from Chris dated February 1995:

Dear Lydie,

I came home this evening exhausted after an unpleasant day of solid visa interviews from 8am to 3pm (7 hours of arguing with people over paperwork uncompleted, expired green cards, etc.), only to have two of my Egyptian employees get in a big fight with each other. Meanwhile, the Egyptians in the tourist visa section, who used to love me, told me I've "changed" and have become a "snob" and "mean". HELP! GET ME OUT OF HERE!!!

At home, I took a nap until the phone woke me up – wrong number – and I immediately fell into a sadness missing you. You're right, it's not fair, we should be together, I need you and it's very hard to be without you. I'm trying to distract myself by writing to family and friends to tell them our news, by tackling the bills that stacked up over the month, by studying Arabic and exercising. But the pain is still there.

I miss you so much I can't tell you, only show you, which I can only do when you're back in Cairo, in my arms again. On a lighter note (laughter helps depression) I'm enclosing a wedding checklist Tom did for Anne's (aborted) wedding.

Love, love, love,
Chris

At this point, Chris was not entirely happy to serve as consular officer at the American Embassy in Cairo. He felt at times as if he was merely a high-level paper pusher. Chris was fighting hard to switch into the political section of the Foreign Service, which he succeeded in doing in March 1995 when he was promoted to political officer in Cairo.

Chapter 13

Wedding Plans

"A successful marriage requires falling in love many
times, always with the same person"

– Mignon McLaughlin

From Chris:

*This is how I will look when I'm sixty, according to my
aunt, who just sent me this picture of Andrew Jackson,
U.S. President. Actually I look like him now, since I
haven't had a haircut in over a month. What do you
think? (You don't have to carry this snapshot in your
wallet. Save it until the year 2020....)"*

The greeting sort of cast a question over my joy. A
sudden, but abrupt departure from the warmth and
confidence that Chris usually projected, was replaced
by wondering and that Chris appeared to be searching
for the future, and involving me in that quest.

The age and the year, 2020, the year he would've
turned sixty, referenced his knack for looking at the
future as though it was only a dream. Perhaps he knew
that he wouldn't live to turn sixty. Perhaps
unconsciously he knew, but didn't consider it as

seriously as he should have.

This whirlwind romance, like a shooting star, you see it, you blink, and it's gone, was taking on massive proportions of love. No longer a whirlwind, it was now, an enduring love that was developing between us. How could I not love him? His charismatic personality, his sensitivity, his energy for life, his intellect, his intelligence, his brilliance, his compassion, his awareness of others and how he was able to express a genuine interest in them and his capacity to love were more than I could have ever dreamed possible from any man. I wanted to spend the rest of my life with him.

I received a letter from him dated February 21, 1995. I sat at my desk. I straightened the petals on a milk white daisy smiling with a yellow face in a vase next to my computer. The steam from a fresh hot cup of coffee wavered and danced in front of me like a ghost flirting with me. A wave of warmth spread over me like a comforter. I felt happy. I felt secure. I beamed with delight. To read this from a man for whom I thought and cared about so much sent vibrations of ecstasy through me. I was where I wanted to be.

Dear Lydie,

I'm sitting in my kitchen sipping coffee early this Tuesday morning before heading to work, missing you, missing you, and missing you. It's very hard to be apart from you. Yet, in a way, being apart from this (hopefully short) period of time is going to strengthen and solidify the feelings we have for each other, I think. It allows us to step back, catch our breath and reflect on our growing (fast-growing) relationship, on the vows we made to each other, and on how we are going to take on the future together. Thinking about us together makes me incredibly happy. You are the perfect woman for me, and I thank God for sending you to Egypt last September!

Sweetheart, I love you and you alone, always and forever,
Chris

Chapter 14

Plans to Meet my Family

"When I say I love you more, I don't mean I love you more than you love me. I mean I love you more than the bad days ahead of us, I love you more than any fight we will ever have. I love you more than the distance between us, I love you more than any obstacle that could try and come between us. I love you the most."

– Unknown

The dripolator whooshed. A new pot of coffee was ready. I could hear it, but it was like a sound occurring somewhere in a distant canyon. Reading the letter was like dancing with Chris; rhythmic and smooth. And that's where I wanted to stay.

At that moment, I smelled the coffee, but it was no longer fresh. The foul aroma of coffee sitting too long on the heat brought me out of my preoccupation with reading the letter. I didn't realize how much time had gone by as I had drifted off into a world detached from reality. Through this haze the burnt coffee snapped me out of it. My mind was churning. I couldn't wait to respond to his letter. So many thoughts and plans bolted through me, I pushed the letter next to my breast.

It was a cloudy day, one of those days that begged for you to be wrapped in a cozy comforter by the fireplace and that was exactly what I was doing. I was watching the travel channel, a program about the islands of Tahiti. Godzilla, my poodle, was curled up and sleeping beside me on the couch. Without warning, he jumped up and barked.

"Shh," I calmed the dog as I pressed my finger to my lips. I put down the book, walked to the kitchen and looked out the window. The postman was depositing mail in the cluster of mailboxes.

When I retrieved my mail, a cold rush of air struck me. I began thumbing through the junk mail and a letter from Chris virtually sparkled in my hand. I rushed inside, closed the door and grabbed a letter opener from my desk.

Letter from Chris dated February 27th, 1995:

Hi honey,

How about getting married in a Coptic Cathedral? We could get some of those monks to chant for us... Your first card arrived yesterday and put me in a great mood for the rest of the day, it was so positive and optimistic. Honey, I can't wait to be married to you, either. And I wish I could be there with you to help you plan and make arrangements. Since it's not possible, I'm putting my faith in you – and I know it will be perfect. You have great talent for organizing events, I've noticed, and this will be the "Event of all Events" I'm sure.

It's hard for me to plan the future with you over the phone. I hear your voice, it makes me miss you even more, and I lose my train of thought! So here are some of my thoughts, while my head is relatively clear. Looking at the calendar, I think it makes the most sense for me to leave Egypt on June 6. That would give us Wednesday, Thursday and Friday to get a marriage license and meet with your business manager and get myself fitted in a white dinner jacket, and do whatever else needs to be done. I'm hoping we can relax a bit on the mornings of the rehearsal dinner and the wedding day (I'd like to take a nice long run!). I think it's important for us to make the dinner and the wedding reception as simple as possible so that we won't have to fret and worry about distracting details, so that we can truly relax and enjoy these events, our guests and each other. I think someone other than you or I should be put in charge of each event, as host (dinner, wedding, reception) so that we can be completely free and undistracted. Particularly on the night of the wedding, we should be free to leave the reception when we're ready and head to the Malibu Beach Inn.

We should think what we want to do in the few days between the wedding and France. I realize that your parents will still be in town. What will we do? I like the idea of combining the baptism and wedding party on the 18th in France. I will request vacation till the 22nd, so I can fly to Cairo on Friday or Saturday, which will give us a week together in Brittany! Sounds good?

Of course, there are lots more to discuss, but these are some of my thoughts for now. We (especially you) are going to be very busy in the next few months juggling work and wedding. In all of this business, don't lose sight of the most important thing: that I love you more than I can tell you, and that I can't wait for us to start our life together, married. Love always,

Chris."

I re-read the words to myself: "I can fly back to Cairo on Friday or Saturday which will give us a week together in Brittany. Sounds good?" He wanted to go to my birthplace because it was where I was born and raised. I had mixed emotions. On the one hand, I was happy he wanted to know more about me, where I grew up, my family, but on the other, I was afraid. What if he didn't like my family? What if he thought we were too different?

On a daily basis, my parents raged at each other in the kitchen. Divorce, I quietly thought. It was a word I had learned at school. My mother's screams were permanent. I quickly learned how to take care of myself and to not draw attention. It was when people forgot I existed that I felt the most peaceful. Drawing and writing became my refuge each day I came home from school. With every scream, I stood alone in my bedroom, in the middle of an explosion, everything flying all around me. I just stood there.

My mother and sister had some special bond to each other, some invisible circle of understanding that they stood inside together, while my father and I were exiled to a duller realm. The threads that tied me to my mother were as frail as a spider's web. I fumbled for something that would impress her and I have been doing so all my life.

Finally, my mother left my father and they divorced. The worst part wasn't all the change my mother brought, but the silence that came with it. Nobody said anything about how we'd lived before. It felt as if the changes themselves had just swept over us like some great wave, flattening whatever we'd once been. Night after night, I lay awake with my eyes burning.

The last sight of my father was indelibly etched in my memory: his white SIMCA had disappeared behind a stand of evergreens. I wouldn't have thought such a vanishing possible, not where my father was concerned. We'd done too many things together and spent all our vacations with each other. My mother was never around.

I didn't know what bothered me the most, the stories that got whispered behind our backs at the supermarket or the silence. Here's what my mother said before she closed the door on my father like a tomb door sealing over the subject of him entirely, "never mention his name again." My mother ordered my sister and I to wipe clean my father from our heads, as if he had never existed.

At the first sign of loneliness for him, I would draw. It helped me to dispel bad thoughts and the deep sadness his absence left behind. At night, I recalled all the amazing stories he used to tell me. My favorite tale was about the magical forest where Merlin's last resting place is. Other nights, I just fell dead asleep lying in Daddy's ghost lap, just as I used to do in his real lap when I was a little girl.

My stepfather's drinking was also bound to me, affecting my thoughts and feelings. The mood in our apartment was tenser than when my parents were together. I guess my mother only knew one way to conduct a marriage no matter whom she was married to. My mother and stepfather fought all the time. With their screams, cursing and fighting, many were the nights when the two of them raged behind their bolted bedroom door, while I crept into the kitchen, gathering up the bottles and throwing them away.

My mother threatened suicide again and again. Her bedside table was a forest of prescription bottles from codeine painkillers to Valium. Throughout the nights when my mother and stepfather were arguing, my mind was racing, looking for a way out.

The phone rang; bringing me back to reality. It was Martine, my best friend and maid of honor. She wanted to have dinner to discuss wedding plans, but my mind was still on Chris's letter and the fact that soon he would meet my dysfunctional family.

Our communications via telephone and letters continued to bond Chris and me more closely together. Even though we were not physically in the same room, there was a connection taking place that, unknown to me at the time, would last for a lifetime.

Chapter 15

Planning for the Future

"It is not in the stars to hold our destiny but
in ourselves."

– William Shakespeare

Letter from Chris dated February 28th, 1995, a card with a beautiful Egyptian couple at home. Under it, Chris wrote:

JCS & LDS having a quiet dinner at home in Cairo (which meant John Christopher Stevens and Lydie Denier Stevens)

Hi honey,

I wanted to send you a note before the post office closes for our 4-day weekend for the end of Ramadan. I'm not traveling this weekend, which is for the best. I need to help my replacement get settled in with his cat; I need to spend a final day in the Consular section finishing pending business and wrapping up loose ends before moving to the political section next week; I need to work on my Arabic while I have the time (before the Vice-President's advance team and my brother arrive and totally occupy me, day and night) and I want to take some time to think about the near and not-so-near future for you and me!

It was wonderful talking to you yesterday evening (remember, the conversation that began in French and ended in English because you couldn't control your laughter...?) I can't bear being away from you! Yesterday I had lunch with the DCM (deputy chief of mission – you met him at Sunny's market) and I asked him about taking off a year without pay. He started laughing, "you just got tenured and now you want to retire?!" Honestly and seriously, after D.C. I'm going to try to get a (paid) year of university training so that we can go to LA or New Mexico (LA is more likely because UCLA has a good Middle East Center).

When I think of us, my mind races forward, into the future. Partly this is because you're not here now and partly because it's exciting to consider our possibilities together.

Honey, I have to run to work now – It's 8:10! I love you – more and more every day. Yours forever and always,

Chris

Sunny's market was a mini-Albertson supermarket where only diplomats went to shop. All of the food in Sunny's market was shipped from the U. S.

Planning, always planning, that was Chris. He had the patent on planning. To plan is to think in terms of the future. To think in terms of the future was something to which Chris paid strict attention, as though it came to him and left him in his seasons of ambiguity and inconclusiveness, just like the Tule fog that settles on the part of California where Chris was born, arriving and departing with the slightest indication of permanency and affirmation.

He defined it perfectly by saying that "when he thinks of us, his mind races forward into the future." He explained that it was partly because I wasn't there with him and partly because it was exciting to him to consider our possibilities together.

Some say a heavy heart means one is melancholy and sad, and perhaps, even depressed. I can't say that I was depressed, but like Charles Kuralt said, "There is melancholy in the wind and sorrow in the grass." I missed Chris terribly. Our time apart drove us both crazy.

Chapter 16

The Date Approaches

"Every love story is beautiful, but ours is my favorite."

– Unknown

L etter from Chris dated March 1st, 1995:

Hi Sweetheart,

As usual, it was very nice to hear your voice last night. Problem is, the more I hear you, the more I want to get on a plane and be with you. This is crazy, this being apart! Most "normal" couples would be blissfully together at this stage in our relationship, working out wedding details and making plans for the future as the Big Day approached. They would be inseparable, visiting friends and relatives together, checking out churches and reception sites, discussing guest lists. Of course, they would have their jobs, too, but at the end of the day's work, they would be together for dinner, maybe a movie, and, finally, bed, where they could hold each other and reassure each other of their love.

Sweetheart, I am trying my best to do all of this from Cairo, and I know you are, too. It's a challenge – but we like challenges, don't we? Just remember that I'm here, always missing you, loving you more and more, impatient as can be to be with you.

Taieb, David (the new Vice Consul), Harry (a Saudi friend of Taieb's) and I went to the Khan Khalili last night to watch the Ramadan crowds. It was wild – more people than I've ever seen swarming in the square in front of Hussein Mosque, through the narrow alleys. We sat and drank Turkish coffee in the supposedly 200-year-old Fishawi's Café, then wandered through the "souk", where I picked out the gold lotus flower for you. Taieb and Harry helped with the bargaining. I hope it will work with the chain I gave you at Christmas.

It's great to have this 4-day weekend to catch up. I'm spending today, the first day of the weekend, at the Embassy clearing out my consular matters – unfinished cases, evaluations for my staff, a couple of reports for Washington. I'll also use the time to work on my Arabic. I'm starting to read text now, and I think about my Arabic language "plan of action" for 1995-1996. I think I'm going to stay with my tutor, and continue to work with texts and songs (the latter one a good source for idiomatic expressions; also, it's good to be aware of who's who in Arab culture).

I received a memo from the State Department yesterday instructing me to bid on jobs for 1996 right now, i.e., my "bid list" of the jobs I would consider for next year is due March 31st. So, in addition to the staff aid position I already told you about, I'll be considering more options, as well – all in Washington, if I can help it. I think it would be a good idea for us to start our life together – and our family – in the U.S., where we can both work (while not being separated by such a long distance when you do have to travel), and where we will have access to excellent medical and other facilities, and where we both feel comfortable. From there, we can plan our next move, east or west, north or south.

    Time to go back to work, I love you more than you think, darling. You are always in my thoughts.

Love,
Chris

Letter from Chris dated March 7th, 1995:

Dear Lydie,

    This will be a short, cheerful card, meant mainly to remind you that you have an adoring fiancé in Cairo who can't wait to wrap his arms (and legs...) around you, and who can't wait to be married to you. Why? You're the best thing that's ever happened to him, and he knows it. He's eager, no, dying to, start his life with you, and he's fed up with waiting. Why wait? Life's too short.

Most of all, he loves you and is committed to you, much more than you might imagine... Kisses and.... Chris

    My, how often has anyone told you that? It came at the right time for it helped melt away all of the stress of the work of the day on the set. Then, as though he was my brain and his brain was mine, he asked, "Why?"

    His answer sends chills through me now, his eagerness to start life with me, his rush, "Why wait? Life is too short."

    Was this a warning in advance of what was to come, a presentiment of the future, a forewarning? How could I have known, when I'm sure Chris didn't either. Possibly, just below the surface of his conscious mind, there was something there that brought these kinds of statements to the surface, possibly not.

Letter from Chris dated March 8th, 1995:

Dear Lydie,

It was sweet of you to call this morning – almost, but not quite, like waking up with you. I'm glad you realize that my morning telephone persona is not my normal persona and does not reflect any lack of enthusiasm for speaking with you. It's just that my brain isn't fully awake yet and it takes longer to send the message to my mouth to start talking!

Three packages arrived today from you – pictures of Egypt, your immigration file, and a nice card. It's just what I needed. This issue of trust, as you mentioned, is very important for us, I realize. I hope I am the most important person in your life as you are in mine. And if I do something that bothers you, please just tell me. Just try to have a talk with me. I respond well to that. Sometimes, no doubt, we will be angry with each other and will raise our voices. Let's just talk like the two adults in love that we are.

If you feel comfortable doing so, you might raise your concerns with my mother during your visit, perhaps in a general way. I know she'll want to talk about our plans – where will we live, will we live together (!), will we have children, what will their religion be – so that might be an opportunity to raise the issues of respect, trust, and fidelity.

Lydie, darling, your concerns are very important to me, our marriage is THE MOST important thing to me, and I will do anything and everything I can to make IT work and YOU happy. Please remember that. I love you now and forever, wherever I am, wherever you are,

Chris

Chapter 17

The Cairo Hollywood Shuffle

"I swear I couldn't love you more than I do right now,
and yet I know I will tomorrow.

– Leo Christopher

Although it seemed like years, I was finally on a plane to Cairo on March 10, 1995. The plane couldn't fly fast enough. Chris was waiting for me at the airport with that smile that lit up the entire world. After hugs and kisses which lasted so long, people were beginning to stare at us, we quickly moved out of the airport.

For the weekend, Chris took me to Sharm el-Sheikh, a city situated on the Southern tip of the Sinai Peninsula at the Hyatt Regency Hotel. Sharm el-Sheikh is the administrative hub of Egypt's South Sinai Governorate. It is known as the City of Peace, which is also its motto. The City of Peace refers to the large number of international peace conferences that have been held there.

We had an amazing time snorkeling in the Red Sea. Before we knew it, the weekend was over. Over wine in a small, out-of-the way, but romantic restaurant, with a single candle flickering between and to the side of us on the table, I noticed a light in Chris's eyes.

"What's wrong, Chris?" I reached across the table and placed my hand on his. He waved his head back and forth, dropped his eyes from mine. It was like he wasn't there.

"I hope this never ends." He looked up at me. The light returned to his eyes. He took my hand and put it close to his heart.

Amr Diab's "Habibi wala wala balo", an Egyptian song, began playing. Chris stood. He took my hand. We walked to the dance floor holding hands. He took me in his arms. We began dancing. The pressure of his body next to mine, his fragrance, his touch, my sense of feeling for him and his taste exploded inside of me as he kissed me at the time we were dancing.

On Monday morning, as Chris was stepping under the shower, he told me I should come with him to the office. I didn't see why I would spend the whole day at his work place, but I didn't argue. Maybe he had a surprise for me. We drove through Nile Corniche Street passing by elegant ornamental palaces and beautiful gardens. As we approached the American embassy, he pulled up right in front of the entrance.

"Come pick me up at 5pm. I will be waiting here." He said.

"What!" I said shocked.

"We are going to be married. You are going to spend over a year here. It's time for you to get used to the driving in Cairo. It's easy. There are only two main streets, Qasr al-Ayni on the east and Nile Corniche on the west. As soon as you see the 6 October Bridge, make a left and a right on Gezira Street. As soon as you see the tennis court where I play, make a left. You will see the building where we live. See you at five," he said as he kissed me.

"As you know people here do not respect red lights, so no need to stop. Just wave at the policeman you will see before you get on the bridge, and point at him the left turn you want to make. There will be a camel next to him, always the same camel. You can't miss it!" He winked at me and leaned to give me a kiss.

I was dumbfounded. I got out of the car, and sat in the driver's seat and dear God I did find our building! And yes, there was a camel next to the policeman! But in the afternoon, I somehow didn't feel quite comfortable enough to drive down to his work. I was afraid of being late, so I found a simple temporary solution: I took a cab.

As the cab pulled in front of the American embassy, right in front of Chris, I smiled at him from the back seat. He shook his head, and sat down next to me.

"Thank you for being on time!" Chris said.

"You're welcome!" I was feeling pretty smug.

As soon as we arrived home, Chris changed into some comfortable clothes and said "Let's go for a drive!"

There I was, back in the driver seat, navigating Chris's car to his work, then returning to his apartment and back to work again, repeating the process until I could drive through downtown Cairo, secure that I could do it on my own. And that was Chris, never giving up, believing in me, believing in us, committed to our life together.

At night we hung out at the Fishawi's café, a famous watering hole for writers, artists, musicians, students and intellectuals. Naguib Mahfouz was the café's most famous regular patron. He wrote parts of his Nobel-Prize winning trilogy novels, "The Cairo Trilogy", in the café's back room.

During the rest of my stay in Cairo, I had become eligible for a green card. To expedite the process, Chris had asked my immigration lawyer in Los Angeles to forward to the embassy all the documentation. I did all the interviews required and medical exams. If I had done it in Los Angeles, I would not have been able to leave the country for six months. There was no way Chris and I could stand to be away from each other for that long. Chris had warned me that after our wedding, I would have to give up my French passport. When you marry an American diplomat, you automatically get a black passport, but you do have to give up your nationality if you are a foreigner. A black passport is only issued to American diplomats accredited overseas and their eligible dependents, and to residents who reside in the United States and travel abroad for diplomatic work.

Now that all my papers were in order, I had to fly back home. I needed to finish preparing for our wedding. I also had to be interviewed at the State Department in Los Angeles. This was required security for the spouse of an American diplomat. Even though we never got married, every time Chris moved up in the diplomatic service, I was investigated as part of the work done for his new security clearance. I never minded this trial burden to smooth the path for a man I once loved and later viewed as my friend. Besides, I am a patriotic American and I believe we need our best people in the world's trouble spots. Chris was the best.

My interview at the State Department took place

in downtown Los Angeles at 8am during a weekday. The view from the 12th floor office was beautiful. From up there you could see the court of justice with hundreds of photographers waiting outside. They were gathered for the murder trial of OJ Simpson.

I sat down in front of four officers. They opened a large file. I was astonished by the first question.

"Do you know OJ Simpson?"

"He's the guy who is on trial for murder," I answered.

"Do you know him?"

"No."

"Are you sure? The officer insisted.

"If you mean, do I know him personally? The answer is no. I just know he's a retired football player and an actor."

"Are you sure you've never met him?"

"I'm sure. I don't care for football."

"Were you on a TV series in 1985 titled '1st & Ten: The Championship'?"

"I was a background actress in it. That's all. No lines. Why?"

"O.J. Simpson was the star of the T.V. series. You never met him?

"Even if I did, I had just arrived in the United States. I wouldn't have known who he was."

The interview lasted a few hours. I was exhausted. The next day, I was flying to San Francisco. I would be staying for the weekend at the home of Chris's mom and stepfather Bob. Chris had asked his mother to host a dinner in my honor. He wanted her to introduce me to his best friends.

Chapter 18

Meeting His Friends in San Francisco

"The way to love anything is to realize that it might be lost"

– G.K. Chesterton

I was waiting for Mary at the gate, and as I didn't see her, I decided to walk outside. She was waiting for me at the curb, and becoming impatient about the delay in my arrival.

"I never go to the gate. I always wait for guests at the curb, it's easier this way!" she explained.

I put my small carry-on in the back seat, and sat in the passenger seat. I was so nervous. I wished Chris could have been here too. I was so afraid she wouldn't like me.

This melancholy passed quickly, but I was reminded of my fear when I spoke with Chris's mother, Mary, one night when we were alone. She explained it as she saw it, from a mother's point of view and as one who had experienced the pain of a failed relationship.

Her first marriage ended when Chris was a teenager, and the experience had a terrible impact on Mary and her family, disrupting the lives of everyone she loved, especially her children. Mary told me that she could see the chemistry between Chris and me but passion like that does not last forever. When the time comes to keep on as a couple, she warned, there must be more, and that was what worried her because Mary believed that Chris and I had very little in common. We came from different backgrounds, different upbringings, different education, different culture, different careers, different everything.

Although I kept my opinions to myself for the most part, I am afraid that I did not react well to what I know now was intended to be kind and intelligent advice. I was young, in love, and single-minded when it came to Chris; we were getting married, and everything his mother had just said was a threat to that. Of course we were different. Did she think I wanted to marry someone whose family upbringing had trained them that family life should be like mine was? I wanted the father of my children to raise them with the same love and devotion that Mary had given to Chris and his siblings. My commitment to Chris was the ultimate statement of respect to her; I wanted to adopt Mary by marrying her son with his family history imbedded in his subconscious. I wish I had been mature enough to say that, or even to understand it. Instead, I just saw her advice as information flowing to Chris as a countervailing current against the river flowing toward our wedding day.

The next day, to prepare for the dinner party, Bob went to the farmer's market, and took me along. Mary stayed home. Twelve people were coming for dinner. She had a lot of preparations to do. Bob and I had so much fun, he was such a gentle soul. When we returned home, Mary had prepared a little lunch and we sat outside for our meal. She had decorated the dinner table with American and French flags. She had done a great job. Mary hosted a wonderful dinner that evening. I loved meeting Chris's friends; my favorite was Austin Tichenor, an actor, like me.

The instant passion Chris and I experienced from the beginning continued to grow as we came to know each other in greater depth. This knowledge came in short bursts: visiting the ancient sites of Egypt and cruising the Nile; drinking tea with the Bedouins in the desert; hiking the sun-drenched hills of Southern California; enjoying the cafes of Brittany. Although our careers forced us to keep our visits short, this was not just a whirlwind romance that is like a shooting star; you see it, you blink, and it's gone.

Chris had a gift for getting to the point quickly, and in no time flat we learned serious things about each other. Anyone in love will tell you that there is nothing more intoxicating than to have the object of your desire learn everything about you, good or bad, and still love you anyway. That was the way things developed for both of us. Ours was becoming a mature love that was taking on massive proportions. We discussed plans to have children who would be brought up in a world Chris could help make a better place.

When I returned from San Francisco, my best friend Martine and I drove to Tarzana to choose my wedding dress. I knew exactly what I wanted, the same thing every girl wants if she's completely honest, to look like a princess. Martine helped me into the dress I had dreamed of since I was a little girl. I climbed on top of a small footstep, and looked at myself in the mirror. As I tried on the veil, I suddenly had a panic attack. I couldn't breathe.

"What's going on?" asked Martine, "are you okay?"

"I can't breathe...I can't breathe. Unzip me, please, unzip me."

When she unzipped me, I just fell on the floor and began to cry. "I have a bad feeling about it....something bad is going to happen." I said, terrified.

Letter from Chris dated March 21st, 1995:

Sweetheart,

You are a remarkable woman, talented, smart, dedicated and self-disciplined in pursuing your goals, loyal, and an excellent and creative cook! You're also sociable and adventurous, and you're a good sport, willing to try out new things (cross-country skiing) without complaint. For these qualities of yours, I fell in love with you and asked you to marry me. Do I find you attractive? Yes, of course. In fact, you are the most beautiful woman I have ever been with, despite what my mother says. I'm not the best looking guy, but all I care about is that you find me attractive and, more importantly, appreciate the more lasting qualities of my personality and character. Over time, they are what count.

I come from a good and honorable family and was raised to be a good and honorable person. I want nothing more than to be the best husband to you and the best father to your children. I am trying my hardest, in difficult circumstances and from far away, to convince you of this. I need you to encourage me and help me by trying your best to concentrate on the wonderful possibilities we have as a couple in love starting a new life together. We need to start living our dream. We both had a taste of that dream while we were in California and Cairo together, and we liked it so much we decided to make a lifetime commitment. I, for my part, am serious about that commitment. I assume you are too. So let's get on with it! With all my love, forever and always,

Chris

The next day, Martine and I went to book the 94th Aero Squadron restaurant to have our reception after the church wedding. It was located in Van Nuys, about a ten minute drive from my home. The restaurant is a replica of a World War I French farmhouse, right next to the Van Nuys airport with a one-of-a-kind view of some of the world's oldest and newest aircraft arriving and departing. I rented the outside patio for our guests. The wedding would be held at the Mission San Fernando Rey de Espana, a beautiful hidden gem. Martine volunteered to have the dinner at her house and a famous Italian restaurant "La Locanda Venetta" was the caterer.

For the rehearsal dinner, Chris had chosen "The Jonathan Beach Club" located in Santa Monica near the Santa Monica pier. The Jonathan Club was founded in 1894 by a group of young Republicans.

Letter from Chris dated March 26th, 1995:

Dear Lydie,
During our conversation last night it occurred to me that the best thing we can do is be together. Because only by being together can we build the mutual trust and

confidence in each other that we need. You were once excited to come to be with me here, but now I feel that you would rather stay in Los Angeles and work. Why do I feel this way? Because, at this point, you know you'll be doing a movie on April 7th at the earliest. You could conceivably come to Cairo now. But you don't want to because there are "other things" you want to work on in case the movie doesn't happen. Up until last night, I thought that finding out the dates the movie would be shot was the only thing keeping you in LA.

As we continued our conversation about our future and the importance of actually living together, you made it clear that you will want to be in LA much more than I had believed up until now. A few months a year? Why? To pay your mortgage and pursue your acting career and this will supposedly continue five or six years into our marriage? It seems to me sweetheart that we're going to have to re-think our plans. If we're having this much difficulty being apart for one month, how do you expect us to deal with even longer separations? My mother was right, we need to live together, and we need to talk seriously about how to arrange our lives so that we can do that. It is unrealistic and unwise to assume that we can begin our life together, apart!

Let's be frank. Your window of opportunity to succeed, as an actress is open now, and will remain open for the next 5 years or so, right? And to make it, you need to be in LA. You can't really accomplish what you need to accomplish from overseas or even in Washington. As for me, yes, the Foreign Service has been an interesting and satisfying career. But it isn't everything. At this point of my life, being happily married to you and starting a family is a higher priority. It won't *be easy to give up this career – as you know, it was my dream to be a diplomat and I enjoy the work and the travel – but I understand that being married to someone means making concessions. I'm willing to make this concession now because we need to be together now and this is the time you need to be in LA.*

Before I make any such move, though, I need to know that you will be 100% supportive, now, while I'm completing my tour in Cairo, and later, while I'm in LA trying to pursue interesting and fulfilling work for myself. Promise me that you won't go off some place far away for six months to shoot a TV series after I've quit the Foreign Service and moved to LA to be with you! That scenario scares me!

Well, honey, these are my thoughts for now. We have much more to talk about. But the main point is that we need to be together.

Your very loving Chris.

P.S. I hope you like the enclosed symbol of everlasting life in gold and lapis lazuli.

A.P.S. I'm very glad you bought the dress and can't wait to see you in it (and out of it!)

A.P.P.S. Kisses, lots, everywhere...

I immediately booked my flight to return to Cairo.

Chapter 19

Alexandria, Egypt, April 1995

"Love is the voice under all silences, the hope which has no fear; the strength so strong mere force is feebleness: the truth more first than sun, more last than star"

– E.E. Cummings

C hris's mother and stepfather, Mary and Bob, arrived in Cairo the first two weeks of April. I was there for a three-week stay. Chris thought it would be fun to go with his parents for a 4-day weekend in Alexandria, an ancient city and major seaport in northern Egypt. Alexander the Great, king of Macedonia, founded the city in 332 B.C. He planned it to be one of the finest ports of the ancient world. It sits in the Nile River delta, on a ridge that separates Lake Mareotis from the Mediterranean Sea. We stayed at the Paradise in Windsor Palace hotel on the promenade of Alexandria's waterfront.

The four of us walked to Pompey's pillar and visited the Catacombs of Kom el Shoqafa with a private tour. This historical archaeological site is considered one of the seven wonders of the Ancient World. It was very educational and a great experience.

On April 15, my birthday, Chris gave me an engagement ring that he had an Egyptian jeweler make specially for me.

On Sunday night, Mary and Bob flew back to San Francisco and the following weekend, Chris took me on a 4-night Nile cruise from Aswan to Luxor to celebrate our engagement. We flew to Aswan, and embarked the cruise ship by lunch. In the evening, there was a welcomed cocktail party by the captain of the cruise ship. The next night was a lot of fun. The party was a "Galabia party" where you dress up in Egyptian outfits and wear the local Galabia. Chris and I loved to dance, and we danced, and danced. We spent our last night at the famous Winter Palace Luxor where Agatha Christie's famous novel "Death on the Nile" took place. After breakfast, we visited the Valley of the Kings and the temple of Queen Hatshepsut.

Early May, I returned home to work on a movie, which was going to be my last. I had made a decision to stay with Chris in Cairo after the wedding until the end of his term. Then we would live in Washington D.C. and see where we would go from there. The only thing I knew for sure was that we were madly in love and being apart was not an option for us.

Chapter 20

Hold Me Tight

"Life isn't a matter of milestones, but moments"

– Rose Kennedy

Perhaps I was too excited, too happy about Chris and the fact that we were getting married. A cloud seemed to hover above me just the same, an ever present menacing presence.

In late May 1995, the phone rang at about 8:30 a.m. I had just fallen asleep after a full night of work on the set of The Assault, a film about a female cop who protects a dead drug dealer's wife from mob assassins. A thought passed through my mind to let it ring. It rang until the answering machine picked it up and I rearranged myself in my bed, nestling more deeply into it. Just as I was beginning to fall asleep, the phone rang again. Strangely, the ringing sound had a sense of urgency to it. It hit me that it could be Chris. I scrambled to the phone.

"Hello?"

"Lydie, it's Chris."

"Hello, skinny chicken."

There was a long pause.

"Yes, I wanted to let you know I arrived back in Cairo in one piece."

Chris had been on a business trip to oversee the arrival of a VIP guest.

"I've been thinking that we should put the wedding on hold." He said.

The call, which had lasted all of thirty seconds, became quiet.

"Chris, are you there?"

"Yes, I'm here. I have to go. If you need to talk, you can call me tonight."

With that, he hung up. There was no goodbye. He didn't say his usual, "Until we meet again." The one making the decision is the one who has to live with it. There is no other choice.

My heart was thudding against my chest like the clonking of hooves that resonates around the ring in a circus. I hung up. I wanted to scream. I wanted to beat the wall with my fists. I wanted to cry. I wanted to run as fast as I could to outrun the pain that was tearing through me. But I knew nothing could change the way I felt so I let myself weep and weep until my body was throbbing with pain. I called Martine. She said she would take care of everything with respect to the wedding. Three girlfriends, each came, one at a time, to stay with me.

Chapter 21

Brittany, June 1995

"The emotion that can break your heart is sometimes the very one that heals it"

– Nicholas Sparks

I prepared to travel to Brittany in June 1995, which was originally planned with Chris. It was difficult because this was the month and year we were supposed to be married. It was my first nephew's baptism. I had to go. I was his Godmother. The day of the baptism was the day Chris and I had intended to celebrate our marriage with my family since they wouldn't have been able to attend the wedding. Before my flight, Chris called me. As he had already put in his vacation time, he asked if he could visit me in Brittany without any questions or commitments. I readily agreed.

When I was a little girl in Brittany, I was ambitious for a different life. I dreamed of America, which I only knew about through films. In the movies, every American was a hero who took risks to help people without a selfish motive. Most of the people I knew in Brittany were not ambitious like me; they mostly looked forward to getting married and having several children, which is pretty much what most of them had done. I wanted children too, but my children would have a father who was a hero and the place to find those was America.

When my parents' divorce became final, my grandmother, an objective-minded woman, a survivor from World War II, asked her niece, Josette, who had married into the high society in Martinique, to raise me as her own child. Her husband was the CEO of the airline in the Caribbean. They had a daughter my age. Her name was Maryline and they thought I would be good company for her.

There I was, sitting in Air France economy class, en route for Martinique. I was 13 years old and being shipped away with a sharp pain in my young heart. That night, looking out the window of the plane, with only occasional turbulence to tease my stomach, I wondered what would become of me. It turned out to be a total disaster. I was miserable. I became their Cinderella and Josette was the wicked aunt. Maryline was the Princess for whom I had to do everything. Joseph, the uncle, turned out to be an alcoholic.

I wrote a letter to my mother expressing to her how unhappy I was. I wanted to come home. I spent weeks praying to receive any day a letter or a phone call with the date for my return flight. But this call and letter never arrived.

A year later my grandmother discovered I was mistreated. She flew to Martinique and took me out of their house. She found a small apartment for the two of us. I was doing very well at school, and she thought I should stay in Martinique and finish my studies without being disrupted.

My grandmother had ambitions for me. She took

me out of Brittany so I could have a better life and find my fortune. On my way to school, one crisp morning, a photographer, a bear of a man with eyes the size of American half dollar coins, discovered me. He owned a professional studio and he hired me as a model. My green eyes caught his attention. They resembled the eyes of Elizabeth Taylor, he said.

Happiness ruled my life. I had very good grades. Living with my grandmother was so much fun. Fashion shows filled my weekends. I was a happy 14 year old teenager, the only white model on the island of Martinique. As soon as I got my degree, my grandmother flew back to Brittany and I flew to Paris.

My modeling career took off, and I began working full time. A career in modeling can offer fantastic opportunities to travel the world, Italy one week, Africa the following week. You meet diverse and interesting people and generate good income. But soon, I became bored. I wanted to do something more challenging. In the back of my mind, there was always this dream of becoming an actor. I moved to Hollywood.

Disappointment cast a shadow across my face when I first stepped on Hollywood boulevard. Glamour had filled my dreams since I was a child but the reality hit me hard. I didn't find a lot of heroes. I did however make friends who were kind, and helped me to adapt to my new country. I learned that if you understand the hard work required to be successful in Hollywood, you need to work there twice as hard as that and you will still be disappointed because everything is subjective. Getting into the movies is nothing like it is portrayed in the movies, but if that's what you love to do, you need to get on with it.

I also wanted to be an American. I never changed my mind about wanting to be one. When you see the things Gaddafi has done, who can deny the virtues of freedom and Democracy? America is my adopted country, and there has been no better day in my life than the day I became a citizen.

But the men I thought were heroes often turned out to be liars. A young girl in America had better learn quickly to tell the difference between an ingenuous declaration of interest and one that is feigned for conquest. Before I met Chris, there were nice men and men who were not so nice, but none cared much about me beyond how I looked. Chris was different. He had a gift for listening because he really wanted to know what made you tick, and to a young woman in love that is flattering at a depth beyond description. Chris's need to satisfy his voracious appetite to know what goes on inside other people, coupled with his talent for listening to them with an ingenuous passion to learn their secrets is what made him one of the fastest rising stars of the foreign service, and that same thing made him the fastest rising star in my life.

Chris met my family for the first time. Being attracted to people, particularly people in other countries, it was relatively easy for my parents and sister to chat with Chris, also because he spoke French fluently. No one asked me why the wedding was cancelled. My family was a family that never asked why. Smiles abounded after a few minutes of exchanging pleasantries.

That was the thing, you know, Chris beamed with charisma. It was affecting. It was like a warm sun layering itself on your skin after a cold day. He simply had the ability to take others by the hand and make them feel like they'd known him all of their lives. Like the diplomat he was, he possessed the skill and tact to interact with others. It was similar to when he convinced me to let him come over. He would explain that we were still engaged, but postponed the wedding to take it slowly.

Trust was the key factor. You felt like you could trust Chris with your life. And many people in North Africa and the Middle East acquired that same trust. Even many people in Benghazi were interacting with him as though he were their best friend. Like Fred Burton and Samuel M. Katz wrote in their book, The Untold Story of the Attack in Benghazi Under Fire, "...He learned the intricacies of the Arabic language and of the Arabic people while teaching them English...Chris, as he was known, was a true Arabist; he was known to sign his name on personal emails as Kress to mimic the way Arabs articulated his name. In the Middle East, Chris is pronounced Kress anyway."

Between times with my family visiting with wine, bread, cheese and grapes, Chris and I did some sightseeing. The first place we visited was La Baule, a beach I used to go to with my father growing up. Chris had done so much research on Brittany; he could have been a tourist guide. We walked hand-in-hand at sunset on La Baule's twelve-kilometer beach, one of the most beautiful beaches in the world. We peered over cliffs and viewed the Atlantic Ocean. We shopped and ate lunch on the Avenue de Gaulle. We were honeymooning without a marriage.

We visited Mont Saint-Michel, an island commune in Normandy, France, one of France's most recognizable landmarks. Mont Saint-Michel and its bay are part of the UNESCO list of World Heritage Sites. More than 3 million people visit it each year. Chris and I "hiked" to the top of the island since it begins with a wide base and narrows as it ascends to the peak where it culminates with the statue of Archangel Michael atop the spirit.

We stayed at a B&B Auberge du Calvaire, in Pont-Chateau, a small village in Loire-Atlantic, not too far from my mother, sister and father. The village was a mixture of old and new houses and buildings. It is located in a site of a passage, on a bend of Brivet, the last tributary of the right bank on the Loire. The bridge that spans it is a stone bridge of a single arch.

Chris and I discovered the shores of Brivet by hiking trails. We rented bicycles and toured the Way of the Cross park where life-size figures, chapels, caves, Scala Sancta, a Jerusalem temple and a museum helped us occupy our time there. The figures were religious, crucifixion statutes. They were everywhere within the village. We would see the people, kneeling and praying before them. Showing respect was of paramount importance. Chris was fascinated about the culture, about people. In all the little cafes we went to, he always started a conversation with whomever was there, always wanting to know more about them.

We agreed when we arrived in Brittany that we would take one step at a time and simply enjoy our time together. We accomplished that, and in more intimate times together, the flame of love burned nearly out of control for both of us. It was a whirlwind of romance for two young people who were both on the ascent in their demanding, albeit different careers.

Chris made sense when he asked that we throttle it back. But that's not what either of us wanted to do when we were together.

Could I have really made the picture I was then filming my last?? My heart knew that was what was required to fulfill our marriage vows, but could I really do that? Could Chris give up his passion for figuring out the people of the Middle East? Thank goodness for our maturity, perhaps old souls at young ages, we were able to turn down the thermostat at an agreeable warmness between us.

Chapter 22

Making Sense of My Feelings

"Love is a promise; love is a souvenir, once given never forgotten, never let it disappear"

– John Lennon

In July of 1995, I flew to Cairo to visit Chris. We went on a long weekend to Moon Beach in the Sinai, one of the most famous places for windsurfing in the world. It's located on the Gulf of Suez just off the main coastal road. We stayed in one of the bungalows with an inverted v-shaped roof that let in the air. The bungalow sat on the beach in a row with several other bungalows lined up in a row. Each bungalow faced the beautiful ocean blue water. We scanned the Gulf from left-to-right and could see only water. To the right were the Sinai Mountains, again, straining our eyes as far as we could see.

Our intimacy clouded any concern I might've had about our relationship. It was confusing in a way to me. How could we be this close and not talk about marriage? Chris's answer to that was for us to continue spending time together and getting to know each other on an even more intimate basis. I guessed that little did either of us realize, that we were enjoying, together what most others would call vacationing, tourism, living aside from the reality of our everyday lives. Marriage and starting a family and what that encompasses was the reality. How could we learn more about each other, unless we were more deeply involved with one another on a daily basis where we would both be going to work every morning and coming home every night to share our thoughts and feelings about what we experienced in our separate days? That wasn't possible unless Chris left his job or I would quit my career.

Letter from Chris dated July 23rd, 1995:

Hi there!

Did you enjoy your week in Cairo? For me, it was one of the best. For once, we were both relaxed and happy, enjoying each other's company.

I know I'm not the easiest person to be with. I think things to death, and if something bothers me, it takes a while for me to say something. It must be frustrating for you, and I'm grateful for your patience. Nor are you the easiest person to be with, at least sometimes. Actually, you are great 99% of the time, and I mean great. You are great with me, you're great with my friends whose judgment I admire and value, and I could tell they were pleased to see you and they like you. You see, it's important to me that you fit in and are comfortable with the type of people I have as friends. The Foreign Service community in which I've chosen to spend the bulk of my adult life, is very tight, more so a small pest. Those with spouses who mix easily with the community are lucky, and their lives are pleasant; those whose spouses don't (e.g., Gregg's and others I know), lead tormented lives, torn by the demands of their hermit spouses and the community. You fit in wonderfully and it makes me happy and hopeful for the future.

Do I still worry about a few things? Like you, I worry a little that we don't include each other in our professional lives, where we spend half or more of our time and about which, naturally enough, we have hopes and dreams. We need to share with each other more. I'm probably the most guilty in this area, I admit, because I assume you won't be interested in my work and therefore don't include you. And then I assume you won't be interested in or really understand my dreams for the future, and so I don't share them with you, and that creates a big gap between us. As for your life, I'm envious when I hear talk about you and Kevin worked on projects together and shared a life in movies and such because it's good to have things in common. Common interests are a bond that keeps couples together. Look at my parents (both sets, after the divorce: Mom and Bob pursuing their musical interests together, my dad and Karen, lawyers, with a common bond and, of course, Hilary), and my now-dead grandparents who traveled around the U.S. for years painting, putting on marionette shows, fixing up their old houses in Nevada City. It's so important to share interests with your spouse; if you don't, only your children keep you together, and you grow apart, as so many couples do after their children leave home.

I love doing things with you, and it's great that you're so enthusiastic. We're both athletic, so there's lots of potential there. (I'm hoping you'll share my enthusiasm for tennis, skiing and windsurfing). We both love to explore; as you know, I can't stay still for long, and I love it that you like going to new places, climbing mountains just to see what's on top, checking out monasteries and mosques and chateaux, fishing for moules, cruising around the desert on a camel and chatting with Bedouins over tea. And I'm very happy that you like meeting people and know how to distinguish between good people and creeps and can handle social situations gracefully. But, like you, I still feel that we're blocking each other out a bit when it comes to our professional lives. I feel still like a stranger to the Hollywood scene, especially when you talk about the stars you're friends with, and I know I need to do a better job of including you in my professional life.

In this, though, it's not the details that are important. It's not important, for example, that you're up to date on the particular policy of this country towards that country. What's important is that you understand basically what I'm up to every day from 8 till 5, and, more importantly, how I feel about my work. It made me very pleased, for example, when you said to me that you worried about my going back to law and later, that you were concerned about whether I could be happy in Washington. I felt like you understood me, and as a consequence, I felt closer to you (in fact, I wanted to continue the Washington conversation but somehow we got onto another subject). Similarly, although I have a sense of what you want from your career, I want to have a better understanding of and feeling for you and your aspirations.

To be a team, we have to have this mutual sympathy. We have great potential because we are alike in so many ways and share a great enthusiasm for what life has to offer. We're very much kindred spirits. But because we were born into different cultures, raised in different circumstances speaking different languages, *and pursued completely different educations and careers, we need to work harder than most to overcome the differences. I want it to work between us I'm going to keep at it. I hope you'll do the same. Love, Chris*

Letter from Chris dated July 28th, 1995:

Sweetheart,

It was so good to talk to you today. I was worried about you and, as I admitted, my imagination started to get carried away, and I started worrying about the shark threat...

Today, Friday, has been a totally lazy day for me. After talking to you, my mind at peace, I decided to read a book and chose Naguib Mahfouz novel about the group of friends who hang out on the houseboat and smoke hashish and talk the night away, escaping their reality of their daytime lives and the new socialist regime of President Nasser. Remember when we took that fateful, midnight drive to Saqqara and almost ran over the man on the canal road? We were just there, you and I! Same road!

Now it's four o'clock and the day is nearly over. No plans for the evening, which is fine with me. Maybe I'll watch the Thin Man. Go to bed early so I can get to the embassy early and catch up on the mounting work. Actually, I've been enjoying the extra responsibility of covering for Barbara while she's gone. Before, I felt under-used and unnoticed, our section is so big, and that has been frustrating, since in Riyadh (my first tour, when I really was junior) I had much more responsibility, and therefore felt more productive and valuable.

As I look at my colleagues who have been in the Foreign Service for a few years longer than I—John

Davison, Barbara, both 10 years—and see what they are doing, which isn't that different from what I'm doing now or I could easily do now, I wonder if I want to spend the next 10 years marching through the middle ranks of the Foreign Service, an anonymous bureaucrat working in the trenches.

Writing reports that, maybe, a few people read in Washington, and taking care of VIP visitors. It's troubling to ponder the near future because I feel I'm capable of doing much, much more (not to be overly immodest!). I feel like I'm going along, doing what's asked of me as best as I can, and doing a good job, but after four years in the business, I understand the basics of it and want to speed ahead, tackle something exciting and high-profile and important, something that makes a positive difference in this world. But the system won't let me because for the next 10 years I will be considered junior or merely mid-level.

Five years ago, in Washington, I spent five dollars on a fortune teller for fun. She said three things, which I still remember today: (1) I will go far away soon; (2) I am better off working independently than in a large organization; and (3) I will settle down with one woman. The first happened, and I believe that the other two are or will be true.

I'll tell you something else that's been on my mind. I miss California—you, my family, San Francisco, Stinson Beach, Lake Tahoe. Sometimes I dream about a life there: you and I, a couple of kids, Godzilla (and maybe a bigger dog for me). A house in the Marin Hills, where we could go hiking on weekends. Ski trips on winter weekends.

Being so far away all the time, I feel sometimes

like I'm missing out on your life, my siblings, and my parents.

I don't know where all this is leading. If you have any ideas or advice, please share them!

Anyway, I'm thinking about you, too (not just myself all the time, as the above might lead you to believe!), and hoping that you'll get some good projects lined up for the year, and that you'll stay happy and continue to want to put up with me! Lots of love, and a big kiss,

Chris.

P.S. Could you please send me a box of that muscle relaxant bath powder you had here? It's not available here. Thanks!

Chris read a lot of books. But his favorite writer was Naguid Mahfouz. The last book Chris read was "The Troubled Man", the tenth and final novel in Swedish crime writer Henning Mankell's series, about a sullen police detective named Kurt Wallander. At sixty, Wallander feels the shadow of his own mortality closing in on him: "creeping up and sticking its claws in the back of his neck." The story is about the reality of politics, a journey into the swamps where truth and lies are indistinguishable and nothing is clear. Chris was unnerved by the downward spiral of the sixty year old investigator, who dives headlong into his work to distract himself from the blank walls of his life closing in around him.

Was Chris troubled like Kurt Wallander? Or was reading about people like this his way of escaping from his own conflict with his work, himself and me? I was never certain. Chris finished reading "The Troubled Man" on September 9th, 2012, only two days before his death. In the six loose pages found on the floor of the mission in Benghazi, Chris had written in his journal: "He's divorced, lives alone with his dog, and slowly descends into Alzheimer's. I'm only eight years from sixty – I need to avoid such an ending!"

Letter from Chris dated July 30th, 1995:

Hi Sweetheart,

I wrote to you yesterday – Friday – the day I stayed home staring at my novel and wondering about the future. Today I got off my (small) butt and took 3 ½ hour walk all the way to the citadel through some old and busy parts of Cairo I'd never seen before, then back downtown to this run-down old English hotel, The Windsor, which has a wonderful 19th century colonial style bar. This is where I am sitting now, quenching my thirst with a cold Stella and writing you this note.

Let me describe this room. Hardwood floors covered with burgundy Persian carpets. Dark wood chairs, tables, couches and bar. Dark wood paneled wall up to about 3 feet, then white walls. Hanging from the walls are antlers from various animals, a large varnished tortoise shell, some 50-year-old black and white photos, and a few oil paintings of Egypt. Around the room in various corners are plants in copper pots. Arabic music plays softly in the background. It's a cozy place, much more comfortable for me then all the 5-star hotels here. I just wish you were with me to enjoy the ambience!

While walking this afternoon, I started day-dreaming about the 2-months gap between the end of my tour in Cairo and the beginning of my job in Washington D.C. in June. I could probably arrange for a "filler" job in Washington, covering for people on vacation. Or... maybe... I could persuade the Department to let me stay here and study Arabic full time for that period. Imagine: 4 hours a day doing Arabic with Madame Faeza, and 2 hours a day of tennis with a trainer at the Gezira Club! Paradise for 2 months! Especially if you could be here then... We could even take a week and go to Sharm Al Sheik or someplace... It would be very flexible, I know, since my predecessor here, Jason, did the same thing.

To do this, I'll have to convince the Department and the Embassy that I'm serious. So, tomorrow, I'm taking the Department's Arabic exam here. The Examiner arrived from Washington last week. Considering that when I arrived I had "0" in Egyptian Arabic, I should be able to get a "2" out of "5" in spoken Arabic. I'm much weaker in written Arabic, but I'll try. Anyway, a score of at least 2/1 (spoken/written) should show them that I've been working on the language since arriving here in March 1994. Sound s good? You know me: Arabic, tennis, coffee "masboot", grilled steaks and wine on the beach, plus you of course! These are my favorite things!

Well, ma Cherie, it's time for me to head back to Zamalek. Let me know how you're doing, what you're up to, what you're thinking, as always.

Love,
Chris.

Letter from Chris dated August 9th, 1995:

Hi Sweetheart,
How are you? I'm at home this Wednesday

morning, the Prophet Mohamed's birthday, sipping Starbuck's (thanks to you) while Egyptian radio plays rock'n roll from the 50's and 60's. Makes me want to get up and start "shaking" my booty but I'd rather shake it with you than by myself. Do you know how to jitterbug? We should dance more, you and I.

My back is getting much better. Time has been the great healer, I think, but I'm going to see a physical therapist next week just to be safe. I hope to learn some daily exercises I can do to reduce the possibility that this will happen again.

It was great talking to you last night. Remember our marathon conversation in which we patched things up? I feel so much better, like we're getting closer to a new level of understanding, and therefore getting closer to each other. We've had a bumpy ride, you and I, but I think it's worth it. My intuition tells me we're good for each other and can have a great life together.

Thinking of you, as always.
Love,
Chris

P.S. I hope you appreciate this "handwritten" note!"

Before I knew it, the holiday season of 1995 had arrived. Joy radiated via colorful and lively Christmas decorations on houses, in malls and on the streets. Holiday music was playing everywhere. Bing Crosby's 'White Christmas,' Nat King Cole's 'Rudolph the Red-Nosed Reindeer' and Joe Williams's 'Let It Snow, Let it Snow.' A different energy vibrated throughout the city. Chris returned for his two weeks of holiday in California. He came to see me.

Each time he entered the room, Chris picked me up and twirled me around, took me in his arms. He kissed me and said, "I love you, Lydie." Literally, I was swept off my feet again and again. We drove to Santa Barbara to spend a week at the Simpson House Inn, an authentic Victorian house. We visited The Montecito Inn, built in 1928 by Charlie Chaplin, his residence.

As before we took many long bike rides along the beach, and enjoyed more unstructured time together than ever before, allowing our thoughts and conversation to drift in and out of light and intimate subjects. Because of the ground work laid to that point, this was our time to bond with each other by exploring details no one would think to ask about, the quirks, sensitivities, and lightlessness that defined us; the touch of a hand, a spoken word, a picture-book gaze, noticing together the smell of a sea breeze, and reading each other's thoughts. A mix of emotion and senses come together to make one, Chris and me.

Chapter 23

Back at Work

"Don't dwell on what went wrong. Instead, focus on what to do next. Spend your energies on moving forward finding the answer."

– Denis Waitley

My Tarzan producers, Max and Micheline, wanted to meet Chris, so they invited us to dinner. I saw this as an opportunity for Chris to get more deeply in touch with people in my field. Because they are producers, Max and Micheline are business people who think and act more like the people Chris is accustomed to being around and are more likely to converse on a subject that Chris would be interested. This is not a knock on my actor friends, but as many who know actors will understand some like to talk about their current film or prospective project above anything else. Once you are accustomed to the culture, no one notices, but I wanted to ease Chris into it. So Max and Micheline were sort of a cross-over.

Max and Micheline have a great home, and it is always a pleasure to be invited there. We sat outside where they have a spectacular view of the San Fernando Valley. Max was barbecuing steaks.

The steady roar of the traffic from the

intersection of the 405 and 101 freeways was distant but close enough to create a constant background for our chat. Chris, the diplomat, had them immediately talk about themselves in no time. Chris had a gift for listening to others. Not only was he interested, but he had the patience to allow people to figure out their own way to say what they mean. He always displayed this attentiveness as though it was second nature to him, and I surmised, why he was so good at being a diplomat.

Max and Micheline discussed a TV series that they were producing. That was after Max's favorite subject, politics, took center stage. General Colin Powell's decision to not run for President, the Oklahoma City bombing, and the trial of ten defendants accused of masterminding and performing the 1993 World Trade Center bombing. Chris and Max talked about Ramzi Yousef, one of the masterminds of the bombing, which was evidently a failed attempt to bring down one or both of the towers. After his death, some theorized the Benghazi attack was orchestrated to capture Chris and exchange him for Yousef, who was tracked down, arrested, tried, convicted and sentenced to two life sentences for his part in the 1993 bombing.

I felt good about how well Chris was getting along with my producer friends when Max suddenly said, "So, Lydie, we want you to replace Catherine Oxenberg in Acapulco Heat." Ordinarily, this would have been a nice role for me and a compliment that producers who worked with me before preferred me over one of their current stars. It had the potential to be good for my career depending on whether the ratings which had been declining would be brought back. But it was a gaffe of the highest order by Max. Because Tarzan was shot in a remote location of Mexico, Acapulco Heat was also being filmed in Mexico. I had talked to Micheline about the problems Chris and I were having with our long distance relationship. This was not how I wanted Chris to learn that I might take another role that would be shot in Mexico.

Acapulco Heat, a TV series about four former CIA agents who fight a secret war against terrorists was scheduled to start filming in Puerto Vallarta, Mexico from mid-May 1996 to mid-December 1996.

I noticed that Micheline kicked Max under the table. "What?" Max asked.

"Ah..." Micheline realized it was too late.

"What is going on with your work, Chris?" Max asked, diverting his embarrassment away from himself.

"Oh, probably, Al-Qaeda is pushing its way to center stage."

In 1996, Al-Qaeda was not the household word that it is today. Some knew it was associated with terrorism, but Chris, of course, was an expert. Max and Micheline moved forward on the edge of their chairs.

"That's scary!" Micheline said.

Chris explained that the origins of Al-Qaeda are traceable to the Soviet War in Afghanistan. It's a multinational, stateless army, radical Sunni Muslims who are calling for global Jihad, but with more threatening implications meaning Holy War, to struggle in the way of Allah and a strict interpretation of Sharia Law, the moral code and religious law of Islam. Al-Qaeda had been designated as a terrorist organization by the United Nations Security Council, NATO, The European Union, the United Kingdom, the United

States, India and various other countries.

Chris took a long draw from his glass of wine. He looked warily at me, then at Max, and returned to the subject I knew was on his mind. "So the filming is going to take about six months?"

Max nodded. He poured some Brut Imperial NV into our glasses, "Yes. We hope to knock it out in six months."

Chris cast a look at me. It was one of longing, perhaps disappointment. I wasn't sure. Later, as we helped Max and Micheline clear the table, Chris said quietly to me. "I don't know how to feel about you being gone in Mexico for six months. I've been assigned to work in Washington D. C. for the next two years. I thought this would be a great opportunity for us to spend more time together."

Somehow, that gave me a feeling of relief. Being in the United States where he was safer, and we were closer in proximity to each other, would be a good thing. I passed a partially empty tray of hors d'oeuvres. Perhaps it was the French in me, I don't know. But how could I give up my job when we were not married and no wedding date was set? If Chris had married me, I would have turned down that job because then both of us would have made a firm commitment. Unfortunately, I know how to say these things now, but I was not as articulate then. I only said that opportunities are rare for actors and I could not pass up a good one unless he had made a commitment to me. Chris only shrugged, but he must have known what I meant.

"I am going to miss you, Lydie. That's all. There's something inside of me that drives me to want to do more about the problems in the world. I sense gravely that I have a future with Al-Qaeda and that I can play an integral role in aborting their terroristic ways, or, at the least, help others from becoming victims of Al-Qaeda."

I put the tray down. I put myself in Chris's arms. "And I love you." We hugged.

"I love you too, Lydie. Thank you for listening. In my position, it's difficult to show my vulnerabilities. With you, it's easy. Thank you."

"You're my Habibi, how else could I be?"

Chris laughed, "And you're the one for me."

"I know, skinny chicken," I said.

"Hey, you two, there's plenty of time for that later, for now, why don't we sit in the den for a glass of wine before you go home?" Micheline said, standing in the doorway. She smiled.

"Sounds good to me," I said. I balanced the tray in one hand and took Chris' hand in my other. We followed Micheline into the house.

I knew we had to be together as much of the time as possible and I had no way of knowing how that could be. Somehow, I knew this would happen. We both would have to choose: Career or us. Or, what we had been working on for six months would go down the drain. We would be separated.

He called me frequently after that. He was somewhat ruffled about his work. He again expressed his frustration over desiring to be more on the front line of where elevated diplomacy was needed. He cited the housing complex in the city of Khobar, Saudi Arabia, where Hezbollah Al-Hejaz detonated a huge truck-bomb adjacent to Building #131, killing 19 U. S. servicemen and wounding 498 people of different nationalities,

Osama bin Laden's message entitled "A declaration of war against the Americans occupying The Land of Two Holy Places" and the Taliban capturing the capital city of Kabul driving out President Burhanuddin Rabbani and executing former leader Mohammad Najibullah, as examples of how more concentrated diplomatic efforts were needed to quell the unrest in the world.

It was my understanding that after Chris told his mother that he didn't want to live without me, she suggested to him to take it slow with me, to get to know each other better, and to get to know my family better before making the big leap into marriage, which I considered good advice. She told Chris that marriage was not meant to be taken lightly, and she was so right. Plus, he had a dream. His dream was to become an ambassador, and to not live his life out teaching Arabic in a school or working in a law firm, which would've made him unhappy, and that it was not fair to ask me to give up my dreams.

Yet always present were the questions I knew were lingering in that talented mind. I had a sense that his family may have raised questions about the wisdom of our engagement, questions that made sense to everyone except two young people in love. There was Chris, a highly educated man of the world, brought up to be a Senator, President of a university, an Ambassador, or maybe even President. A man like that, gains strength from a woman who is similarly educated and one who can help him get to the top and stay there. Not a woman like me. Or so I thought when I wondered why Chris was reluctant to make a commitment.

Chris's family had been wonderful to me, but they must have counseled him about how quickly we were moving forward with our engagement. I can only speculate that they must have advised that he would be better off with someone with a few degrees under her belt and, that beauty fades; breeding matters when one rises to the top. But it was not Chris's nature to listen to such warnings.

More likely, I thought, Chris was torn by the demands of his life's work. One day he came clean and told me I was right. Chris had become an expert in diplomacy within the most difficult area of the world imaginable, the Middle East. Not only is it a violent place, but the circumstances for the wives of diplomats were becoming increasingly worse at many of the postings considered the best for a rising star like Chris.

We talked about this many times. Chris was always logical, never anguished. Optimistic by nature, Chris said there was no reason why two people who love challenges could not solve this one. After all, we both had careers, and it would not be necessary for me to be in the Middle East when I was shooting a movie or TV series. He too would spend time in the United States during his Washington postings. It all sounded so easy. But it wasn't. What about the children? We both wanted them. What kind of life could we give them? Chris spoke seriously about striving less aggressively to achieve the top rungs in his career. I was shocked that he would even suggest it because I knew by then how passionate Chris was about pursuing his dream of helping the people of the Middle East in order to further American interests for the right reasons. But love can make anyone stupid. So I am ashamed to say that I eagerly encouraged him in this path. I wanted him to do anything that would keep us together even though I now know that it would have been exactly the wrong thing for him to do.

Letter from Chris dated March 13th, 1996:

Dear Lydie,

It was great to get your upbeat and newsy letter. Ours must of crossed in the mail. I wanted to respond and to see if you planned to be in LA or nearby in April, since I would like to see you when I come home.

Your new Tarzan show sounds interesting, but very far from the original concept. Where's the jungle, Jane?

I've been in touch with Fatima and Aziz who kindly showed my Dad and Karen around and gave me good advice on how to deal with a local doctor who was overcharging me for a couple of back therapy sessions. They are looking forward to seeing you in Florida.

Sweetheart, I'm looking forward to see you next month, hopefully.

I miss you,
Chris

Nostalgia can never replace what was. Being together, touching each other, feeling each other, smelling each other, tasting each other, and hearing each other are real interactions between a couple. It was at this point, as it was so many other times during our relationship that I decided I had to elevate my mind above my heart and be strong through this until I had completely exonerated it from my emotions.

Fatima was a tour guide that Chris hired to show me around each time I visited Cairo while he was at work and also when his family was in Cairo. She was outgoing and pretty and her love for Egypt was expressed through the passionate manner of her presentations to tourists. Although Fatima impacted essentially the same information on every day tour, none sounded rehearsed; she was so engrossed in her stories that they sounded original every time. Fatima was married to a doctor. In January 1995, she said to others about Chris and me, "They're going to get married." She spoke French fluently.

Letter from Chris dated June 9th, 1996:

Dear Lydie,

I'm sorry I didn't make it to LA to see you before you go off to Mexico. I was very tempted. How was the trip to San Diego? You must be very sad to let go of Godzilla, but at least he'll be in a good place.

It's been foggy and raining here, off and on, since I arrived, but cool enough for me to take regular 3-4 miles runs – my health has improved dramatically since Cairo. And while I'm still a skinny chicken compared to some, I've put on some weight and, according to Tom, look stronger than when I first arrived. Cairo took its toll.

Good luck down South shall I write to you at your San Fernando Valley address?

Love,
Chris.

Even though he expressed a desire to see me, I could see what he meant by Cairo taking its toll. He wasn't sure about himself regarding me anymore. It was reflected in his focus on his health rather than his focus on the decision he had to make so that we could be together.

Sometime during the six-month shoot, Chris was assigned to work in Washington D.C. for the next two years. He never did come to see me in Mexico while I was working on Acapulco Heat. He was working. It happens, you know. Indecision is an example of trepidation.

Chapter 24

The English Patient

"The man falls out of the sky, clinging to his dead lover.
They are both on fire. She is wrapped in a parachute
silk and it burns fiercely. He looks up to see the flames
licking at his own parachute as it carries them slowly to
earth. Even his helmet is on fire, but the man makes no
sound as the flames erase all that matters – his name,
his past, his face, his lover..." from the movie The
English Patient.

– Michael Ondaatje

In a letter from Chris dater December 2, 1996, he
explained that he'd just seen The English Patient.
He thought the love story was like ours, an
impossible love. He admitted that he identified with the
excerpt from the script. He articulated his thought that
the passage was a metaphor for the love we had
between us, the chance we had to be infinitely together.
His cousin, Matt, told him the book was also really good
and he was going to buy it.

I had never experienced this side of Chris. The
passage read like a form of depression to me. I didn't
want to accept the idea that Chris was depressed. He
never came on that way unless it was something he hid
behind his curtain of secrecy, another side of him about

which no one had the slightest awareness.

He shared with me that he had just finished yet another Naguib Mahfouz novel, Respected Sir, about a poor civil servant whose sole goal in life is to rise to the position of Director General of his department, and be addressed as "Respected Sir", passing up love, marriage and family along the way. He achieves his goal, finally, but at great personal sacrifice.

Was this a harbinger of things to come? I didn't know. I didn't want to think about it. I just wanted to be with Chris. He went on in his letter talking about playing tennis with ambassadors and letting them win. It was a dichotomy of sorts, depression and happiness, winning and losing. How to define Chris was becoming more difficult now. A slight fading away of the beaming California man with a sunshine smile and a sensitive heart for everyone was quietly and slowly dissolving into darkness.

Before Christmas 1996, I travelled alone to my family home in Brittany. Chris travelled alone to San Francisco to be with his family. I was always thrilled to go home to be with my family, especially in 1996 when Dylan, my two and a half year-old nephew was there. I grew so fond of him. We put up a Christmas tree and stayed home. Wine and food dominated our holidays and I showered Dylan with Christmas gifts.

While dinner was being prepared, we gathered in the dining room to enjoy a semi-sweet white wine, Vouvray, and help control hungry family members, I added warm and crispy feuilletes d'escargots (snail pastries) to go with the Vouvray. French people really do eat snails, and wash it down with good French wine during the holidays.

Our Christmas Day meal consisted of goose, a seafood platter and oysters. For dessert, we ate the Buche de Noel, known here as a Christmas log. My sister and brother in law had prepared the meal, while I played games with Dylan.

My mother, my stepfather and my sister, her boyfriend and his parents laughed and talked about past Christmases together, while my sister and I chatted about movie stars. But no one mentioned my aborted wedding. I missed Chris so much too. Soon, it was time to leave and say goodbye.

Chapter 25

Los Angeles/Washington D.C. 1997-1998

"Hold fast to dreams, for if dreams die, life is a broken-winged bird that cannot fly"

– Langston Hughes

Slowly the pieces of the jigsaw puzzle are falling into place now that he is dead. Chris loved me for sure. He also loved his job and he was ambitious to succeed at it. But here's the piece I did not have before Chris began to see his role in the Middle East as destiny; it was more than mere ambition to be good at his job. Even if I could give up my career were he to marry me, which I thought was realistic, would that even be enough freedom for Chris to pursue this newly perceived destiny? Like others who have made an indelible mark on history, Chris was beginning to believe that he was beyond being able to live the normal, peaceful, safe and secure life of a normal American man. There was something far more compelling "out there" that he had to pursue and catch before his time ran out.

As the pieces fell into place, I became increasingly aware of the man I loved, the man I wanted to marry and the man whom I wanted to be the father of my children. Chris was pursuing a vision, and I understand that as he took the steps necessary to fulfill that vision, he would find no room in his life for a wife and children, no room for me. This vision of course took him to Tripoli as the American Ambassador to the Libyan people and then to Benghazi. Chris served his country by helping Libyans live their newly acquired freedom productively and live in the decency of a democracy. For that, he sacrificed everything else in his life, including the plans we had made.

The sense of doubt and indecisiveness raised its hard-featured head once again in Chris's letter, although I sensed this, I stubbornly kept trying.

Letter from Chris dated February 14th, 1997:

Dear Lydie,

Happy Valentines Day from your skinny cold chicken in D.C.! Wish I could be there with you to wine and dine and romance you the way you deserve to be! Love, Chris

Inside was a sullen-looking photo of the United States Capitol in the blizzard of 1966. It looked isolated, lonely and empty. Sometimes I think too much. Someone said that many creative people are like that. I don't know, but I have to react to what I see, in my way. A touch of fantasy here, but what the heck, fantasy can serve as a replacement for reality, just to meld the longing, the desire, the love into a getaway world where giants are elves and clover is a bed of sweetness that carries you far above the heaven most of us have been taught to believe exists, when, in truth, heaven is what we believe it to be, no more and no less.

During the next two years, I flew to Washington D. C. to visit Chris several times. On each visit, he had planned a different agenda for us to follow so that we could get in as much time doing things together as possible. That was Chris. Although it was our plan to interact in this way so that we could get to know each other in ways that were essential to our goal of getting married, it was obvious to me that Chris was changing his mind about marriage even though he was just as affectionate toward me as before. Somehow, I knew in my heart that it was never going to happen, and if I knew it, Chris knew it too. We still had that connection, that loving bond. What was going on with Chris on the subject of marriage had nothing to do with the reason we wanted to get married in the first place. That's why neither of us wanted to give up the precious moments we were having together. But ever so slowly, it began to occur to us that moments were all we would get. So without discussing it, Chris and I had decided to live in the moment, for the moment was all that we had. And it wasn't half bad.

There are so many monuments and memorials in Washington D. C. Chris alphabetized them. Each time I visited him, we went to the next of those listed for that particular visit. We started by seeing the World War II Memorial, working our way "up" through the alphabetized list that ended with the African American Civil War Memorial and Museum.

This took the better part of the next two years as Chris worked at the State Department. We spent lots of time together while Chris served sequentially as a staff assistant in the Bureau of Near Eastern Affairs, then

Iran desk officer, and finally, as special assistant to the Under Secretary for Political Affairs, Peter Tarnoff. These were jobs for a young man on the rise toward becoming a United States Ambassador.

When I visited, it became clear to me that all of these jobs were stressful for Chris. He relieved his stress by going on a run, playing tennis, and touring Washington, D. C. with me. I could feel the edge in him, but he was usually able to relax with vodka and peanuts, or a nice glass of wine. When nothing else worked, resting in each other's arms almost always did the trick. Perhaps the edge was something that stalked him, something that he kept to himself, perhaps his fear of the unknown, the future and how risky it would be to become a U. S. Ambassador in the Middle East. At some point, I believe, Chris sensed that his destiny did not allow him the luxury of the family we had planned together, and buried in places he had yet to acknowledge, he knew we must eventually part. I'm not sure when he knew.

Letter from Chris dated October 21st, 1998:

Dear Lydie,

This card reminded me of you. Thanksgiving in NYC?

-Chris

A card with a picture of a glass of Grand Marnier and the words French connection contained so few words but so many expressions. The past, the present, the future, all wrapped up in less than twenty words, a photo and a mix recipe for a drink. It caused my heart to ache. I wanted to reach across the country and touch his face. I wanted to tell him how much I loved him, and how much I yearned to be with him.

I never had a chance to persuade Chris to abandon the idea that he could not marry if he was to fulfill his destiny because the incessant periods of physical separation ripped apart our relationship. One of us always had to be somewhere urgently, especially when the other had just opened time to be together. These frustrating separations were our relentless enemies. They destroyed a relationship that once seemed inseparable. Focusing on the present and the vitality of my life helped cushion the blows of being apart, but how does one fill the void that absence of love creates? Does it harden one's soul to compensate for the emptiness?

Chris and I spent time together in New York during Thanksgiving in 1998. We stayed in Long Island, in Merrick, at the home of my friends, Marie and Tom. We also went to see Bob's sister's home in the city. Those experiences were heart-warming. We were not engaged anymore, but we were still seeing each other. Chris and I were still a couple. We were interacting with friends and family, it was a coming together that I hoped would lead to the resolution of our desire to be with each other on a regular basis.

Chapter 26

When Life Doesn't Line Up

"Ever has it been that love knows not its own depth
until the hour of separation"

– Kahlil Gibran

L etter dated October 31st, 1999:

Dear Lydie,

*It makes me very sad to have to send you your
things. We're no longer together, but I miss you terribly.
You brought so much love and commitment to our
relationship. You tried so hard. We both did. But it just
wouldn't work. The shoe didn't fit, no matter how hard
we tried to make it fit. I hope you'll remember the good
times we had together, and not the difficult moments. In
a lot of ways, we are good together. Certainly, the
passion is there, and that is very important. And I
admire you so much for your talent, your energy, and
your determination. You are a remarkable woman, and I
feel lucky to have known and loved you (actually, I still
love you), but sorry to conclude that we can't make a life
together.*

This is a difficult time for both of us, given the

great expectations we both had. We're strong, though, and we'll get through it. I hope that you find happiness in your life. Although we may be apart, there will always be a place for you in my heart.

Love,
Chris

Chris had embraced the idea that he had to choose between his career and me. We argued about it all the time. Looking back, he may have been right, but I could not possibly accept it at the time. I wanted to be married to Chris, and I can make anything work. That's what the stubborn French girl said, and no one could make her believe anything else. This idea of Chris's destiny is only clear to me now, while I grieve his death. On October 31, 1999, Chris made the decision to end our relationship.

The "touch" Chris exhibited via letters and pictures was a cornerstone of who he was: multi-dimensional. He always came at you from a variety of directions, all well intentioned, just so there could be peace and light and love. Oh, if only it could have worked out for us...

Perhaps nothing is ever quite as painful as getting over your first love. It's not just any love. We thought we'd spend the rest of our lives with each other. We had made plans for the future. We had loads of jokes and memories of the time we spent together. Now that it was over, I was scared that I would never find anyone to ever replace Chris, or maybe just afraid that I wouldn't ever be as happy with someone else.

It was not easy going on with our lives without each other. In so many ways we were perfect. There was, and continued to be, something magical between us.

Nighttime was the loneliest. It was so hard to sleep, or get back to sleep when I woke up in the middle of the night. I opened my eyes and thought it was a bad dream, but it wasn't a dream. It was reality. There were days I felt emotionless, and days overly emotional. I let myself cry, and cry, and cry. I knew I would heal with time, and I realized it would not happen overnight. Was he feeling the same way?

Chris struck again with a short, but informational letter.

Letter from Chris dated January 22nd, 2000:

Hi Lydie,

Of course, when I read the enclosed I immediately thought of you. Seems like a good time for a film about her life, if you haven't already done it. How are you? You made me famous in our embassy in Paris and at the State Department with your "Je suis celibataire depuis 2 ans" interview in Dimanche magazine! I'll be going overseas again this summer, to Jerusalem via two years of Arabic language training in Tunis, starting this August. So if you're in the mood for a Mediterranean vacation, you'll know where to find me. Meanwhile, I'm still in D.C., enjoying the snow and ice... Take care, Chris"

Hedy Lamarr had just passed away and he had enclosed a Washington Post obituary on the famous actress.

Letter dated April 9th, 2000:

Dear Lydie,

An early birthday card greeting since malheureusement (a French word that means unfortunately), I won't be able to wish you a happy "25th" anniversaire in person on The Day. So, we both advance a year again, and what a year it has been! Personal highs and lows, career success, lots of frequent flier miles... you and I have been through a lot together, despite the short time (like a shooting star bright across the night sky). Now, I hope, we're both back on earth again, feet on the ground, perhaps a little bruised but on the whole healthy and a little wiser. And whatever happens, you can be sure that there's a skinny Californian chicken in D.C. who cares very much about you and hopes that only good things come your way.

Love,
Chris.

Card from Chris dated June 5th, 2000:

Hi,

how are you? What are you up to these days, besides your quick trip to S.F.? I would of course love to see you but won't get to California till July 8th or so. Where will you be in July? Should I stop by? Chris

Reading the penetrating words cast a sharp pain through my heart like pushing an awl into it. Why? Why? Why? Why did we come together and flame out only to end up apart like this? To transcend the problems, to make choices that are contrary to the way one is, to resist the changes that will take place in one's life, requires the capability to elevate one's consciousness to the point where you can make clear and sound decisions that benefit everyone involved. Then again, each one of us is human and we possess the strength that is level with our life experience, no more or no less.

I watched a bird take flight, and then grown smaller and smaller in a bright, blue sky. A black speck now, it soon disappeared, and I was left to wonder how my life would've been with Chris if only he would have trusted that he could have had it all, career and family.

After our break-up until after September 11th, 2001, Chris always sent me a Valentine's card, a birthday card, holiday season card, and a card that somehow always arrived on or about June 10th of every year, close to the date we were supposed to get married in 1995.

The last time I physically saw Chris was after 9/11 in 2001. He was in California and called me. When I answered, he said: "Well, hello! Can you guess who it is?"

I replied: "Skinny chicken!" That warm voice he had on the phone. He wanted to see me. It was on a Sunday. I didn't want to start right back at square one, or all the work I did to get over him would be wasted. But I couldn't say no.

At the time, I was doing a play in Sherman Oaks in which I had the role of Greta Garbo. I invited him to see the play. After the play, we went across the street of the 99 seat theater to have dinner in an Italian restaurant. I also invited my friend Myeva, who was playing my best friend in the play, the role of Salka Viertel.

After the dinner, he walked me to my car and

asked me if he could spend the night at my home, as he hadn't reserved a hotel room. I said yes. Back at my house, we opened a bottle of wine. He said he wanted to start a relationship again, said he was still in love with me, and he was missing me a great deal. I had reached a point of wanting to get over Chris. At first it hurt so much. I was being torn between the desire to move on, and the hope that we would eventually get back together. I thought about it for five minutes. I told him I didn't want to start a relationship with him again. There was too much pain. I showed him the guest bedroom.

The next morning, he wanted us to go for a walk in Malibu. Maybe it was his way to rekindle our love for each other, to bring up the good memories we had together. I had a meeting in the morning with Billy Zane for a movie project. I told him we would go early in the afternoon when I returned from my meeting. But when I came home, he was gone. He had left me a note on my dinner table, and my key was underneath the mat by the front door.

Afterward, we cut off all communication with each other. It was harsh, but it was the only thing that would work. We couldn't be friends while attempting to get over each other. I was losing the best friend I ever had, the only person who truly understood me.

I had a long road ahead of me. No miracle cures. Time would heal. I hoped to find love again.

Chris,
Grass Valley,
California,
1961

Me
Brittany,
France
1965

Me and my dad,
Brittany, France
1965

Chris as editor of The Piedmont Highlander Newspaper, 1977

Me as a model, 1978

Me as Nicole in the TV series Acapulco HEAT, 1996

Me as Hedy Lamar, shoot in San Francisco, 1995

Me as Jane in the TV series Tarzan, with actor Wolf Larson

Chris at 34.
Cairo, Al Ahram
newspaper party
where we met,
September 11,

Me on
Lake Nasser,
Egypt, 1994

Night of the
party for
Al Ahram
newspaper,
Cairo,
September 11,
1994

Chris in
Southern
California
1995

Chris in
Lake Tahoe;
December
1994.
I took this
picture of
him.

Chris
teaching
me how to
Cross-
country
ski in Lake
Tahoe,
December
1994

Me and my
dad, 2014

On a cruise
on the
Nile River,
April 1995

Visiting
Alexandria,
Egypt with
his mom
Mary,
and his
stepfather,
Bob,
April 1995

Chris at 40

Me at 40,
Paris, France

PART TWO

Chapter 27

Undying Friends

"Surround yourself with the dreamers and the doers,
the believers and thinkers, but most of all, surround
yourself with those who see the greatness within you,
even when you don't see it yourself"

– Edmund Lee

In 2000, Chris travelled to Tunisia to continue studying Arabic at an Arabic language school. He was among 12 students in the class and another student was Mark Shapiro who now serves as senior Turkey desk officer. According to Shapiro, he and Chris learned to speak Arabic well but still needed more studies to learn how to become fluent in the written language. Together they travelled to Damascus to engage in four more months of grueling Arabic studies. Afterward Chris was sent to serve as political officer in Damascus, Syria.

An article in the New York Times stated the following: In Syria in 2001 and 2002, he [Chris] courted Iraqi exiles before the American overthrow of Saddam Hussein's government the next year. When the embassy in Damascus, Syria, held his farewell party, he [Chris] insisted on it being in a disco and invited all the Iraqis, who were fractious even then. "This was probably the only time the Iraqis sat at one table—before or since," said a State Department diplomat who served with him.

From 2002 through 2006 Chris served in Jerusalem as political officer at the American consulate dealing with Palestinian affairs. His tour took place during the second Palestinian 'intifada' (uprising) when Palestinians were blowing themselves up on Israeli buses and Israeli troops were raiding West Bank villages. In a bit of unorthodox public diplomacy, Chris and a junior officer went outdoors during a rare snowstorm and started lobbing snowballs at each other. Young Palestinians and Israeli border guards on opposite sides of the divide joined in. It broke the tension, at least temporarily. His amusing behaviors were misleading however, because Chris rapidly became one of America's savviest envoys.

Daily Telegraph reporter Harry De Quetteville who was also living in Israel at the time said, "Chris Stevens was the antithesis of the ruthless, bombastic, culturally insensitive American diplomat whose stereotypical image haunts the pages of bad fiction and, all too sadly, the minds of his atavistic killers. Though it may sound a do-gooding cliché, he was concerned principally with the welfare of the people in the countries where he served, and considered the advance of that cause to be of the greatest benefit to both sides."

From 2006 to 2007, Chris worked as a Pearson Fellow with the Senate Foreign Relations Committee and Senator Richard Lugar. In 2007, when the United States resumed relations with Libya, Chris was appointed deputy chief of mission and later as the chargé d'affaires at the embassy in Tripoli. During his first tour of Libya, Chris worked on rebuilding the embassy which had been vacated during the Libyan insurgency. Chris's fate was sealed from this moment forward.

The silence remained between us for seven years until May 28, 2008, when Chris sent me a request on LinkedIn.

Lydie, Bonjour... it's been awhile. Hope you are well. I'm in Tripoli, Libya, of all places. I see you are still in LA, producing (acting in?) films?

Chris.

I responded immediately and we reestablished a friendship that lasted until the day he died.

In an email dated May 29th, 2008, Chris wrote to me:

Well, well... Sounds like you are doing great, with your directing and writing. Are you still living in Sherman Oaks or did you relocate? I recall last time we met you were looking for a new place to live. Berlin and Paris and NY, too? How glamorous! Libya is the opposite of glamorous, I must admit, but it's unusual and challenging, so I'm happy. The weather is hot, as you might imagine, but they have miles and miles of beaches. And they have a tennis court. I found a good trainer and have already played in two international tournaments and did pretty well (even got on Libyan TV!) Lots of years to cover, but I won't try to do that here. Suffice to say that there have been ups and downs, like everyone else. Curious to hear your news. A big hug for you (and a kiss, after all these years!)

Chris.

PS, I am attaching a picture of me at the famous Roman city of Leptis Magna, with my "true love," Medusa, who just celebrated her 1,400th birthday. Hey, we're all getting older, right?

Chapter 28

First Feet on the Ground

"We are ready to sacrifice our souls, our children and our families so as not to give up Iraq. We say this so no one will think that America is capable of breaking the will of the Iraqis with its weapons"

– Saddam Hussein

On April 5th 2011, Chris slipped ashore undetected from a Greek cargo ship at Benghazi. Having been appointed the United States envoy to Libya, he was there to set up a U.S. liaison office to the rebels, working out of a hotel room. Inspired by the so-called 'Arab Spring' in other Middle Eastern countries, rebels in Libya had begun armed conflict against their longtime leader Muammar Gaddafi beginning that February. Chris's assignment was to be the first American diplomat to make contact with the newly constituted Libyan Transitional National Council.

The Council had been appointed to coordinate all rebel activity against the central government, which was led by the despised dictator, Muammar Gaddafi, who still held the upper hand from his stronghold in Tripoli. Chris's job involved providing reliable information and thorough analysis upon which Washington could formulate policy. Chris soon convinced Washington that the Transitional National Council had the political bona fides to pick up the pieces after Gaddafi's 42 year rule.

Chris understood that he had to express empathy in a genuine way. He defied the stereotype of an American diplomat who was equal parts arrogant and ignorant. Chris was honest and human. Once, during his first tour in Libya when Muammar Gaddafi was still in power, he grabbed the camera from a Libyan intelligence goon who had been tailing him. With an enormous smile, he snapped the guy's picture before returning the camera. The lanky Californian could be both charming and disarming, even as he made his point.

Chris worked hard to forge stronger links with the rebels and to better understand the different factions fighting against Gaddafi. America trusted Chris Stevens to meet with this new council and initiate a dialogue. It was not known who the members of the rebel council were exactly. In all likelihood, some of them were sworn enemies of the United States and could easily decide to murder Chris. And then there were Gaddafi's forces that surely had spies everywhere in a country where Gaddafi, whom Ronald Reagan nicknamed the 'Mad Dog of the Middle East,' had ruled with brutality for decades.

Enemies were everywhere and if Chris was lucky, perhaps a few friends. All Chris had to do was persuade them to be loyal to the United States, which had not exactly been generous with its military support. Bruised from interventions in Afghanistan and Iraq, the United States had stepped back to 'lead from behind,' allowing Britain and France to take the initiative in NATO's military support of the Libyan rebels.

When Chris slipped into Benghazi from the Greek cargo ship, US officials regarded him as a highly knowledgeable hand when it came to Libya. Colleagues dubbed him the expeditionary diplomat. He had been posted in Libya in 2007, as deputy chief of mission, then at the embassy as chargé d'affaires, Tripoli. In August 2008, Chris was tasked with preparing Secretary of State Condoleezza Rice for her upcoming visit with Gaddafi. In 2011, WikiLeaks made public Chris's previously classified preparation, along with the fact that Gaddafi harbored a huge crush on Secretary Rice, which she described as "weird and a bit creepy."

During my journey, I learned that the trust shown in Chris's talent, knowledge and ability in Libyan affairs by our national leaders was shared by his co-workers. Gregory Hicks told me, "Chris was to so many of us [in the Foreign Service] the example of what we signed up to be. He was the archetype. Chris and Robert Ford are the nonpareil, the two archetypes of the American diplomat who we all want to be. The people who mastered the foreign language, the people who had no problem being around for hours and hours in coffee shops and in people's homes and offices, within the whole culture and conversing and learning and exchanging views in the language of that culture." If Chris had not been killed, he said, "Perhaps the Middle East would be a little better off than it is today. My guess is that Chris would now be in the Near East Bureau, you know, working on the big issues of the day, which would be Syria and Iraq."

For Chris, the Greek cargo ship experience probably was a great adventure. He must have appeared like a modern-day Lawrence of Arabia; a tall blond blue-eyed gentleman sailing to Benghazi and arriving incognito aboard a ship, surrounded by 14 armored vehicles and 17 American soldiers carrying automatic weapons.

Chris and his small team of diplomats and volunteers from the United States Agency for International Development (USAID) arrived in Benghazi not long after U.S. and NATO airpower had pushed Regime Forces out of the city and further south to the cities of Brega and Ajdabiya.

James D. Foggo, RMDL, USN, who served as operations officer for the Libya Campaign wrote in his blog for the U.S. Naval Institute, "For my part, I believed we were overlooking one big factor in our planning: A personal interaction with the guy we were going to have to extract. So, I arranged a phone call with Chris. I just wanted to tell him one thing: "Chris, if you need us, the Navy and Marine Corps have got your back."

Foggo continued: "Since no American military boots were allowed on the ground in Libya during the operation, and since we were just amassing Intelligence, Surveillance and Reconnaissance assets, we were starved for real time eyes-on-the-ground information about what was going on. Chris was a wellspring of knowledge. He was direct, candid and incredibly informed. When I hung up, I told VADM Harry Harris, then the Sixth Fleet Commander–Boss, Chris Stevens is one phenomenal guy. Now I know why State sent him!"

Chris's reports back to Washington encouraged the U.S. to support the rebel council, which the Obama administration officially did in July 2011.

In a New York Times Magazine article dated November 14, 2012, staff writer Robert F. Worth wrote: "In Benghazi, Stevens and his team became de facto participants in a revolution.

They moved into the Tibesti Hotel, a 15-story tower overlooking a fetid lagoon, where the lobby was a constant, promiscuous churn of rumors and frenzied meetings among gunmen, journalists and spies. Unlike all his previous posts, there was no embassy to enclose him. His room then was a dilapidated sixth-floor suite full of gaudy gilded furniture and a four-poster bed; he seemed amused to know that Abdullah el-Senussi, Gaddafi's right-hand man, had often stayed there. Stevens reveled in his freedom. He met people in their homes, ate with them on the floor, Arab-style; cell phone photos were taken and quickly shot around the Internet. He went running every morning and often stopped to chat with people on the street, to the dismay of the security officer who ran alongside him. In August, after Islamists killed a top rebel commander, Stevens drove out to eastern Libya's tribal heartland and spent hours sitting on the beach with five elders of the Harabi tribe. The men ate grilled lamb and talked in Arabic, sipping tea. Stevens did not push them for answers. He was building connections that would pay off someday."

Chapter 29

Chris's Confirmation Hearing

"Learn from yesterday, live for today, hope for
tomorrow. The important thing is not to
stop questioning."

– Albert Einstein

On Tuesday, March 20th, 2012, the U.S. Senate
Committee on Foreign Relations in Washington
D.C. met, pursuant to notice, at 2:50 pm, in
room SD-419, Dirksen Senate office building,
Honorable Barbara Boxer presiding. Senators
Menendez, Coons, Udall, Lugar and Risch were present.
They met to consider John Christopher Stevens to be
Ambassador to Libya.

Opening statement of Honorable Barbara Boxer, U.S. Senator from California

"John Christopher Stevens recently served in
Benghazi, Libya, as the special envoy to the Libyan
Transitional National Council, or TNC. Prior to this
post, Mr. Stevens served as the Director of the Office of
Multilateral Nuclear and Security Affairs at Department
of State.

Mr. Stevens is a career member of the Foreign

Service. He joined the State Department in 1991, and I am very proud to say he is a Californian. Mr. Stevens, you have been nominated to be the U.S. Ambassador to Libya. And like so many, I watched in awe as the Libyan people fought with tremendous courage to bring an end to the brutal regime of Colonel Muammar Gaddafi.

But now the Libyan people are facing another extraordinary challenge, building a functioning government, civil society from the ground up. If confirmed, we hope you will be able to help convince the Libyan people to lay down their arms, to put aside their differences, continue the hard work of building a new and better future for Libyan men, women, and children."

Opening statement of Honorable Richard G. Lugar, U.S. Senator from Indiana

"Well, thank you very much, Madam Chairman. I join you in welcoming our distinguished panel. I would like to extend a personal welcome to Chris Stevens, who spent a year on the committee staff in the 2005-2006 timeframe.

He then went to Tripoli as deputy chief of mission during reopening of diplomatic relations with Libya after twenty seven years. For much of that tour, Chris was the chargé d'affaires and lead interlocutor with the Gaddafi government. Chris was assigned again to Libya exactly a year ago, but this time his post was to be in Benghazi as the special envoy from our government to the Transitional National Council.

Chris has served his country for 22 years on

issues related to North Africa and the Middle East. He served as a Peace Corps Volunteer in Morocco, and as a Foreign Service officer, he served tours in Saudi Arabia, Egypt, Syria, Jerusalem and Libya.

Madam Chairman, I valued Chris's knowledge and insight while he was on my staff, and also have appreciated his willingness to offer counsel on the situation in Libya over the past year. I am very pleased the President has nominated a man whose substantive knowledge, experience, and respected leadership are so well suited to this posting."

Statement of John Christopher Stevens, of California, to be Ambassador to Libya

"Madam Chairman, Ranking Member Lugar, and Senator Coons, thank you for the honor of appearing before you today. I wish to thank the President for nominating me to serve as Ambassador to Libya and for the confidence that he and the Secretary have shown in me. It has been a great privilege to be involved in U.S. policy toward Libya at different points over the past several years, as Ranking Member Lugar has noted. I first served in Tripoli in 2007 in a country that was firmly in the hands of an oppressive dictator.

Last March, I led a small team to Benghazi as the special envoy to the Transitional National Council. It was a time of great excitement as the Libyan people first experienced freedom, but it was also a time of significant trepidation for what might come next.

Should I be confirmed, it will be an extraordinary honor to represent the United States during this historic period of transition in Libya. Libyans face significant challenges as they make the transition from an oppressive dictatorship to a stable and prosperous democracy.

Colonel Gaddafi deliberately weakened the country's institutions, banned even the most rudimentary of civil society organizations, and outlawed all electoral activity. During his rule, corruption was rewarded, initiative was discouraged, and independent thought suppressed. To change such a system will take time and much effort.

Libya's new leaders must build democratic institutions from scratch, consolidate control over militias, ensure that all Libyans are represented and respected in the new government and dispose of the country's oil wealth fairly and transparently.

Despite these difficult challenges, there are some signs of progress. The interim government is paying salaries and providing basic goods and services to the Libyan people. It is reconstituting government ministries, preparing for elections in June, and ensuring that Libyans throughout the country are represented by the new government.

Libya's oil production, which is important in stabilizing world oil prices, is expected to reach pre-conflict levels by the end of the year. It is clearly in the United States' interest to see Libya succeed as a stable and prosperous democracy. Such an outcome would enhance our security and economic well-being; through for example, security cooperation in the region, steady oil and gas production, and opportunities for U.S. businesses as Libyans rebuilt their country. It would also serve as a powerful example to others in the region who are struggling to achieve their own democratic aspirations.

There is tremendous goodwill for the United States in Libya now. Libyans recognize the key role the United States played in building international support for their uprising against Gaddafi. I saw this gratitude frequently over the months I served in Benghazi, from our engagements with the revolution's leadership to our early work with civil society and new media organizations. If confirmed, I would hope to continue the excellent work of Ambassador Cretz and his team in assisting the Libyans with their transition and forging strong ties between United States and Libyan officials, business communities, students, and others.

As you know, the administration has proposed a modest package of technical assistance for Libya during the transition period. It is fair to ask why the United States should provide any assistance at all to Libya, given the country's wealth. Libya's new leaders have often stated that the country intends to fund its own operations and reconstruction, and they are, in fact, already doing so, tapping their petroleum revenue and other assets of the previous regime.

It is in the U.S. interest to fund a limited number of activities that address immediate security and transition challenges. These U.S. funded programs are aimed at preventing weapons proliferation; providing advice to the interim government on elections and other transitional governance issues of immediate concern; and promoting a vibrant civil society. A limited investment in the immediate transition needs of Libya now will pay dividends for a lasting U.S.-Libya partnership in the years to come, and will help ensure that Libya contributes to regional stability and security.

Thank you and I look forward to your questions."

Senator Boxer: "I want to ask a question about Libya. And thank you for taking on this challenge. This is not an easy time to go over there. I am just very proud that you have accepted this challenge. As one who backed the decision to engage in the U.N. no-fly zone, obviously, there is much to be proud of – the successful overthrow of Gaddafi and watching the Libyan people try to build a new government, a civil society from the ground up.

But I want to ask you about something troubling—the militias that refuse to disarm. Today, there may be up to 200,000 fighters in Libya who are refusing to lay down their arms despite pleas from the highest levels of the Transitional Libyan government. What plans has the Libyan government outlined to demobilize militia groups? What steps has it actively taken to implement those plans? What assistance has the U.S. government offered? And just overall, are you concerned that armed militias could play an intimidating role in the run-up to the planned elections in June?"

Chris Stevens: "Thank you, Madam Chairman, for your kind remarks and for your questions. This is probably the most serious question that Libyan authorities face right now, the issue of disarming and demobilizing and reintegrating the militias into Libyan civilian life. As you said, there are thousands and thousands of militia members scattered around the country and based in the capital and Benghazi as well. The Libyan authorities are grappling with this issue as we speak. In fact, they already began some months ago in the final days of the revolution. And the plans that they have put together have a goal of incorporating some of them into the security forces, be they the police or the military, and some of them into civilian life, hopefully, the private sector or perhaps other civilian government jobs.

In terms of the steps they have taken, they have coalesced around more than one plan. I have to say it is not as organized as one might like it to be. But the steps that they are following involve, first of all, registering the names and personal data of the militia members, and they have made quite a bit of progress on this: Long lists of these people, who they are, where they are from, what skills they have, and where they would like to fit into Libyan society. So this is the first step. And then, beyond that..."

Senator Boxer: "So, if I can interrupt? So, they want to reintegrate them? Because that is important, remember in Iraq what happened? Said no more Baath Party members of the militia, and they just turned them all away, and that started a whole what I would say "civil war". So that is very interesting. Thank you for that information. Continue."

Chris Stevens: "They are very mindful of the Iraq experience, and in fact, some of them use the phrase 'debaathification' as something that they would want to avoid. So just to finish this thought, the next step would be to actually hire portions of them into the security services and the military and then direct others into the civilian areas of life, including training.

Now, what are we doing about this? Well, the U.N. is taking the lead role in organizing the international effort to help many of these areas, and one of them is providing advice and assistance based on other experiences that countries like ourselves and the EU members have had around the world with similar situations. And so, we and the EU and other countries are working with the U.N. to provide assistance in this area, mainly in the form of advice."

Senator Boxer: "Thank you."

Senator Menendez: "Mr. Stevens, I have the families of 32 of 189 Americans who died on Pan Am flight 103. And as someone who has been supportive of our efforts in Libya, but I also believe it is very important, as I told the Prime Minister when he visited the committee, that in order for Libya to be able to move forward in its future, it must reconcile events of the past. And there are still many of these families who believe that justice has not been achieved for them. And while their loved ones can never be replaced, a sense of justice is desired and is ripe.

So my question is have you met or will you meet with the Department of Justice about their open Pan Am case before departing for Tripoli? And is it your understanding of U.S. policy to continue to actively pursue information about the bombing and other terror attacks orchestrated by the Gaddafi regime against U.S. citizens?"

Chris Stevens: "Thank you, Senator. The Pan Am 103 bombing was a horrific act and one that we cannot forget, and I certainly will keep it on my mind when I go to Libya, if I am confirmed.

I do plan to meet with the Justice Department officials in the coming days and weeks to discuss their case, which I understand is ongoing, and I am referring to the criminal case. And we have, as you know, raised this issue with the interim Libyan authorities, including during the visit of the Prime Minister of Libya a week ago or so when you met with him. So, Senator, absolutely, that would be on the top of my list of issues."

Senator Menendez: "So you will visit with Justice before going to Tripoli?"

Chris Stevens: "Absolutely."

Senator Menendez: "I appreciate you say you will keep it on top of your mind. I would like it to be one of your priority items in your agenda."

Chris Stevens: "It certainly would be, sir, if I am confirmed."

Senator Menendez: "Thank you very much."

Senator Udall: "Mr. Stevens, one of the programs that Gaddafi left behind was a huge water project known as the Great Manmade River. The goal of this project was to bring water to arid regions of the country and improve the agricultural capabilities of the county. What is the current status of this project? I know issues have been raised in terms of sustainability and whether this was a good project or not. Is the United States supporting the project? What are you doing in terms of environmental review if you are going to work to move it forward?"

Chris Stevens: "Thank you for the question, Senator.

The Great Manmade River Project, of course, was one of Gaddafi's legacies. It was actually begun before he came to power and got its start during oil exploration by an American company that stumbled on some water out in the desert in southern Libya. Since then it has provided a good portion, if not majority of Libya's water supply. Critics say that it is expensive and that it is a waste that they are trying to grow agriculture in areas which they shouldn't. People on the other side say, well, it is a resource they have, and why shouldn't they use it?

During my time in Benghazi during the revolution, it largely continued to work unaffected. There was a brief interruption at one point, but they have since made the repairs that were necessary, and now it continues to provide significant water to Libyans, both to cities and to farmers. We are not providing any sort of assistance at all to this project. It is strictly funded by the Libyan government, and they are using foreign contractors from Korea and Turkey and other places to help them.

Chapter 30

Additional Questions and Answers Submitted for the Record

"Yesterday is history, tomorrow is a mystery, today is a gift of God, which is why we call it the present."

– Bil Keane

Senator Lugar: "Please provide detail for the committee on the Libyan fiscal situation, particularly as it pertains to assets frozen and unfrozen around the world."

Chris Stevens: "Libyan authorities recently released the 2012 budget, which totals 68.5 billion LYD (or $55 billion). According to local press reports, it is a balanced budget, which relies heavily on oil revenues. In December 2011, the U.N. delisted the assets of the Libyan Central Bank and the Libyan Arab Foreign Bank. The United States also removed sanctions on those two government entities, leaving very few assets frozen under U.S. jurisdiction. Those assets are now available to Libyan authorities. The Libyan government has not requested that sanctions be lifted from the two remaining government entities listed at the U.N., Libyan

Investment authority (LIA) and the Libyan African Investment Portfolio (LAIP), pending its reorganization of their management structures."

Senator Lugar: "You are heading to an Embassy which was greatly damaged in the revolution. Please describe the Department's plans for rebuilding your Embassy and facilities. Has the government of Libya made any offers to assist in the reconstruction? What money has been designated and what planning has been done by OBO (Bureau of Overseas Buildings Operations)? What is the plan for consulates, if any?"

Chris Stevens: "Due to the level of destruction at the former Embassy compound, the Department has established an Interim Embassy until such time as a New Embassy Compound can be built. At this time, the government of Libya has not specifically offered to assist in the reconstruction of the U.S. Embassy but is engaged with the Department of State on the issue of land acquisition as we conduct initial site searched for the New Embassy Compound.

OBO is working closely with Department offices and other agencies that will be working in the Interim Embassy to ensure that the facility adequately meets security and the operational needs of all tenants. Evaluation teams have traveled to Libya to review existing facilities to ensure proper planning and usage of the facilities. Funding for building the Interim Embassy will come from all agencies that will make use of the facility. Within the department, the Bureau of Resource Management is fully aware of the financial needs associated with the Interim Embassy.

Currently, the Department is staffing a small

office in Benghazi, Libya, that is responsible for monitoring the pulse of political action in eastern Libya. However, once national elections have taken place, the Department will reassess its utility."

Senator Lugar: "Will assignments for Tripoli staff be conducted in a normal fashion, or are they being given shortened assignments and special incentive packages?"

Chris Stevens: "There is a temporary incentive package for personnel assigned to Tripoli now and in the 2012 summer and winter 2012/2013 cycles. The Department will return to a 2-year tour of duty when security and living conditions normalize. Embassy Tripoli is operating in extremely difficult conditions. U.S. government employees are housed on a secure compound, two to four persons per bedroom and up to four people per bathroom depending on the number of personnel. All movements off-compound must be coordinated with a secure package. Due to the limited living space, employees are not permitted to take unaccompanied baggage, household effects, consumables, or personal vehicles to post. The incentives package entails 1-year assignment, with 35 percent hardship pay, 25 percent danger pay, and the provision of two Rest and Recuperation (R&R) trips or one R&R and two Regional Rest Breaks (RRB). This package is being reevaluated as the situation in Tripoli changes and will be adjusted based on the overall security, stability, and openness of the situation."

Senator Lugar: "Gas prices for many Americans currently top $4 per gallon and worldwide the price of a barrel of oil is $107. You stated in the hearing that Libya expected to be back to prewar levels of oil production by the end of the year, but would you provide more details on the status of the Libyan production and export capacity? Are American firms back fully, and if not, what reasons are they expressing to you?"

Chris Stevens: "Even though the United States imports little oil from Libya, restoring Libya's participation in the global oil market will have the effect of stabilizing supplies which is important for our ability to access supplies at an affordable price—a key element of our energy security policy. Libya is making significant progress in restoring output to its pre-crisis oil production level of about 1.6 million barrels per day and is currently producing over 1.4 million barrels per day, according to the Libyan authorities.

Most of the U.S. firms involved in production in Libya have reopened their offices in Tripoli and are taking steps to resume normal operations. U.S. firms have identified both security and logistical constraints in their meeting with us and we have engaged with the Libyan authorities on these issues."

Senator Lugar: "If you were addressing American businessmen, what would you want to tell them about opportunities in Libya? Do you expect to have a Senior Commercial Officer from the Department of Commerce as a member of your Country Team to assist American companies interested in investing in Libya?"

Chris Stevens: "As Ambassador Cretz has so often stated—and the Libyans have repeated publicly—Libya is now "open for business." U.S. Embassy Tripoli, in coordination with the Department of State's Bureau for Economic and Business Affairs, established a series of sector-specific teleconferences which provide a "direct-line" for American companies to the U.S. Ambassador. The Embassy has completed six sector-specific teleconferences to assist the American private sector to identify commercial opportunities in Libya. These teleconferences have focused on sectors including infrastructure, security and healthcare, and have had upward of 100 participants per call. This program has been such a success that Secretary Clinton has asked the Department of State to expand it, worldwide. If confirmed, I will continue the program in Libya, in order to keep U.S. companies abreast of all commercial opportunities emerging with Libya's political and economic transition.

The demand by the U.S. private sector for commercial opportunities in Libya is big, and it's only getting bigger. There is also tremendous demand in Libya for goods and services produced by U.S. companies. Broadly, there is great need for infrastructure, information and communications technology, oil and gas services, power generation, transportation products, and infrastructure, including rail. I refer to you to the Department of Commerce for details on their staffing plans in Libya and elsewhere. If confirmed, I certainly would want Department of Commerce representation in the Country Team at Embassy Tripoli."

Senator Lugar: "What, if any role will U.S. assistance play in the security sector reform elements you discussed in the hearing?"

Chris Stevens: "The United States will continue to play a supporting role to the transitional government of Libya (GOL) in security sector reform. We will work with the U.N. Support Mission in Libya (UNSMIL) and international partners to coordinate our assistance, and if confirmed, I will assist in these efforts.

Libya's Ministry of Defense (MOD), Ministry of Interior (MOI), Ministry of Justice (MOJ), and intelligence services are being reconstituted in the wake of the revolution. Currently, there is minimal absorptive capacity within the GOL for robust security sector assistance. The greatest need is for technical expertise to help the GOL shape its security apparatus and to assist GOL efforts to disarm, demobilize, and reintegrate (DDR) revolutionary fighters.

UNSMIL and our international partners have taken the lead in assisting the GOL to implement a DDR process. UNSMIL is diligently working to facilitate GOL security sector coordination through the creation of a Libyan MOI to assist in standing up a GOL police force. Jordan has signed a memorandum of understanding (MOU) with the MOI to train 10,000 new police cadets in basic police curriculum. The Libyan MOD has launched an assistance coordination mechanism to keep track of assistance to the armed forces, avoid duplication and identify gaps. The French have conducted joint maritime training with the Libyan Navy. Qatar and the UAE have committed to MOD assistance, but have not had any real engagement or response to date.

UNSMIL is also working closely with the GOL to

coordinate the DDR process. The GOL and UNSMIL report that Libya's Warrior Affairs Committee had registered 148,000 fighters to date. Assisted by the international community, the GOL has announced a 3-year plan to integrate 25,000 revolutionaries into the regular military and 25,000 into the police forces. The remaining revolutionary forces will be reintegrated into civilian life through initiatives to develop small and medium business enterprises, or through new educational and training opportunities.

We aim to support these efforts by deploying targeted security sector assistance that will focus on bolstering GOL capacity and leveraging international assistance. In April, the Department's Export Control and Related Border Security (EXBS) program will fund the deployment of a team from the Bureau of International Security and Nonproliferation, Office of Export Control Cooperation, and the Department of Homeland Security, Customs and Border Protection, to conduct a 1-week consultation and basic enforcement training overview for Libyan MOI, MOD, and Customs Officials who will be leading the efforts to develop and integrate Libya's border security forces and integrate rebel fighters into the Libyan forces.

Over the summer, the Anti-Terrorism Assistance (ATA) program will send an assessment team to evaluate the current capacity of Libyan law enforcement units that perform counterterrorism functions and to examine whether and how we can begin ATA training in the coming year.

In late March, we will deploy a security sector transition coordinator to U.S. Embassy Tripoli who will coordinate and report on these border security and MOI training efforts. We are also using the congressionally notified Presidential Drawdown authority to provide nonlethal personal equipment to the MOD as it forms a national military capable of providing protection to the civilians and civilian populated areas within Libya.

Additionally, funding from the FY 2011 Middle East Response Fund (MERF) will be used to support a DDR advisor in Tripoli whose focus will be on reintegrating militias into civilian life through advising the GOL on creating employment and education opportunities for former militia fighters."

Senator Lugar: "Libya faces significant needs as it develops its civil society in this period of transition. The United States is prepared to assist with training and technical assistance. With oil production of 1.4 million barrels per day and expected to increase, to what degree is Libyan able to use its own national assets to bear the costs of this development?"

Chris Stevens: "We do not have detailed information on the exact expenditures of the Libyan Government in various sectors, including in civil society. We, however, do have evidence that the government has taken steps to ensure it has funds to meet the country's needs including by working to get the production of oil back to prewar levels. The government has also passed a budget of $55 billion, helping to ensure that ministries can pursue reform, renovation, and capacity-building projects.

The Libyans have repeatedly stated they want to pay for the reconstruction and reform of their country and promote civil society. In the near term, however, Libya is spending the majority of its resources on ensuring that salaries are being paid and that basic services are provided to the Libyan people. The United States and the international community are currently filling short-term gaps in priority sectors and funding actors that we believe should receive assistance independent of the government, including certain civil society groups and the media."

Responses of Christopher Stevens to questions submitted by Senator Barbara Boxer

Senator Boxer: "According to the United Nations, as many as 6, 000 detainees, about three quarters of those arrested during Libya's civil war, continue to be held in prison facilities run by individual militia groups operating outside the control of the government. International human rights groups including Amnesty International and Human Rights Watch have provided deeply disturbing evidence of what appears to be widespread abuse. If confirmed, how will you work to promote the humane treatment of prisoners in Libya?"

Chris Stevens: "I share your concern regarding continuing reports of arbitrary detention and prisoner abuse. I, too, find these reports deeply troubling and, if confirmed, I would continue to raise the issue at the highest levels of the interim Government of Libya, as I understand Ambassador Cretz and his team are currently doing.

Ambassador Cretz and his team have stressed the importance that the United States places on protecting human rights and the specific need for the Government of Libya to get all detainees and detention facilities under central government control as soon as possible. Our Embassy has also joined with other like-minded embassies and multilateral organizations to press these points, a practice that I would continue if confirmed.

The interim Libyan Government has made positive statements regarding its respect for human rights, condemnation of torture, and commitment to consolidating control over militias and detention centers, including informal sites where most allegations of mistreatment originate. We recognize that this will be an important step in ensuring humane treatment and in establishing registration and review processes in accordance with international standards, but the government needs to go further.

If confirmed, I will continue the close contact with the Ministry of Justice that Ambassador Cretz and his team have maintained. I would continue to emphasize that the United States stands ready to assist Libya as it seeks to develop new Libyan judicial and corrections systems that meet international standards by ensuring due process and protecting basic human dignity.

I would also continue to promote continued Libyan Government collaboration with the International Committee of the Red Cross, the Office of the U.N. High Commissioner for Refugees, and the International Organization for Migration which can provide technical assistance on protection of migrants and refugees as well as visit detainees, as our Embassy in Tripoli is already doing."

Senator Boxer: "In November 2011 I held a joint Foreign Relations subcommittee hearing with my colleague Senator Casey to examine the role of women in the Arab Spring with a specific focus on Egypt, Tunisia, and Libya. If confirmed, will you commit to working to help ensure that women play a strong, meaningful role in the political process in Libya and that their rights are fully protected?

Chris Stevens: "Libyan women played a vital role in the 2011 civil uprising and revolution that toppled Moammar Qaddafi. During my time as the Special Envoy to the Transitional National Council in Benghazi last year, I had the privilege to meet and work with many inspirational Libyan women supporting the cause of the people. If confirmed, I am committed to ensuring that women are encouraged and supported to play a strong, meaningful role in the political process in Libya and that their rights are fully protected in law and practice.

After 42 years of Qaddafi's dictatorship, Libyans have very limited experience with democracy and an open political process. Most candidates, both men and women, have no experience in the democratic realm and the challenge for the Libyan people will be to create a national dialogue in which all of Libya's diverse population can participate. A number of Libyan women activists are already urging strong women's participation in decision-making bodies and speaking out about the importance of electing women in the June elections. Under the electoral law passed in February of this year, 80 of the 200 delegates to the interim National Congress will be elected from lists submitted by political parties. Party lists are required to alternate between male and female candidates, a process known as the "zipper quota". Observers hope that the law will lead to increased participation by women in the government. A similar system was used in Tunisia, based on that experience, some electoral experts expect that around 10-15 percent of the Parliament will be comprised of Libyan women. This is still far lower than the women's percentage of the population but it's a start.

Numerous women's groups and women-led organizations have emerged in Tripoli, Benghazi, and outlying areas since the beginning of the revolution. A few of these organizations, most of which are led by women who have management experience working for international corporations or significant experience outside Libya, have successfully initiated or completed projects that include a women's rights march to advocate at the Prime Minister's office, national conferences for youth and women, a reconciliation campaign, the establishment of women's centers and holding fundraising events. Many of the women's organizations are loosely constituted groups with limited organizational capacity to plan or implement activities beyond charity functions but have expressed a desire to expand their activities. Both experienced and inexperienced organizations have begun approaching our Embassy in Tripoli for assistance with conferences to inform women about their rights and prospective roles in elections, constitutional development, civil society, and the economy.

I believe that the United States can help to provide targeted amounts of technical assistance to help these organizations build up their capacities in these nascent stages, as we are already doing through

USAID's Office of Transition Initiatives (OTI) and the Middle East Partnership Initiative (MEPI). I understand that the United States is one of the only donors currently providing support to these local grassroots women's organizations and, if confirmed, it's a priority I will continue to emphasize.

USAID/OTI has already been providing support to women-led organizations as well as others that have significant female participation. USAID/OTI is currently planning initiatives such as: holding a national workshop on women in elections that will train women to educate people in their home communities about the importance of having female representation in the constituent assembly and constitutional commission; developing a toolkit of materials to be used in multiple training opportunities; and replicating a successful women's center that aims to facilitate engagement among women's NGOs for the following projects: a constitutional workshop for government, political, and civil society leaders; a public awareness campaign to promote reconciliation, unity, and forgiveness as a means to move the nation toward a peaceful transition; and a youth training session that included a field visit to a local women's NGO.

MEPI programs in the sphere of women's empowerment include: a program to help Libyan businesswomen and women entrepreneurs connect with their counterparts throughout the region; a National Democratic Institute-led candidate training for a group of aspiring women politicians; and a small grants and capacity-building program for several small women-led or women-focused civil society organizations. These organizations are working to combat discrimination against women, encourage the participation of Libyan housewives in the political process, support the advocacy efforts of women with disabilities and establish a women's training center.

I applaud and support all of these programs and, if confirmed, would like to continue similar programming in support of women's political participation and the protection of women's rights in the new Libya.

As promised during his confirmation hearing, Chris met with the families of the victims of Pan Am flight 103 on April 27th, 2012, via video. I have seen powerful evidence that Chris did far more than think about this important act of terror, and I had hoped to display some of that touching evidence here. But a lawyer for the families asked me not to include it because someone told him that Chris "never had a fiancée," which is a shame because it deprives the public of another warm story about Chris. It is, however, not the worst that has been said of me since I began my journey, and the story tells itself after a certain point.

Chapter 31

The Ambassador

"Be the Ambassador for what you stand for"

– Nisha Moodley

On May 14th, 2012, Chris was sworn in as United States Ambassador to Libya, achieving his crowning moment.

"Why do you want to go back?" I emailed him in May 2012.

"I know I can make a difference there." He said.

The trial of Saif al-Islam Qaddafi, the former ruler's son and political heir, will be a pivotal test for Tripoli. As a former lawyer, Chris was aware of the need for real justice under the government elected this year, rather than a repeat of Qaddafi's murder after rebels caught him trying to escape through a sewer pipe. But Chris also understood the sensitivity about any U.S. attempt to help write a new Libyan constitution. He instead favored American assistance on the basics of rule of law, such as training police on collecting credible evidence, judges on courtroom procedures, and prosecutors and defense lawyers on honoring the restrictions as well as the responsibilities of the law. He wanted Libya to become a model for a region prone to capricious justice.

Chris was a natural gentleman, as though from deep within, he had an innate and genuine ability to like and care about others. His scholarly intellect neutralized any feelings of inferiority one might naturally experience when you were around him. He had an infectious warmth and compassion, and he demonstrated genuine concern for everyone he met. Of course I knew he could make a difference in Libya. I had seen him in action when we were in Cairo.

In a video produced by the State Department, Chris expressed his passion to help the people of Libya. He said he was looking forward to a stronger relationship between both countries. He also spoke of how he had had the honor to serve as the US envoy to the Libyan opposition during the revolution, and was thrilled to watch the Libyan people demand their rights.

"Now," he concluded, "I am excited to return to Libya to continue the great work we started. Libyans are going through difficult times, challenges. I want peace in this part of the world."

During previous times he had spent in Libya, Chris said that he enjoyed listening to stories from people who were "old enough to have traveled and studied in the United States back when we had closer relations." "Those days are back." He said.

Chris commended the high number of Libyans who were currently applying for Fulbright grants to study in the United States, and the pledges being made by Libyan health care workers to form partnerships between Libyan and American hospitals.

In advance of arriving at his post, Chris completed the two weeks of State Department mandated training in emergency self-defense. During this training Chris learned how to handle himself in case of a convoy attack, kidnapping, or other hostile events. He learned how to speed away in a car in reverse, how to maneuver a moving car from the front passenger seat should his driver become incapacitated, and how to fire a pistol.

Since Chris's death, the State Department now requires 10 weeks of mandated training in emergency self-defense instead of two. Chris's Deputy Chief of Mission in Libya, Gregory Hicks told me, "It's still not enough. You have to know how to use a weapon, but you have to be mentally prepared and able to use a weapon if you must. You have to look at that person and that heart that is beating twenty feet away and pull the trigger. You've got to put the first bullet in the heart and then the second bullet in the head."

Chris left for Libya on May 24th, 2012. He had a deep affection for the Libyan people in general and the people in Benghazi in particular. He also knew Libya as well as anyone in the U.S. Foreign Service, most likely even better. He would soon learn much had changed in Libya from the time he left as Special Representative in November of 2011 until the time he returned as Ambassador.

In the months leading up to the Benghazi attack, the instability and violence in Libya in general and toward American assets more specifically was significant. In the aftermath of the 2012 Benghazi attack, investigators identified more than a dozen violent events in Benghazi during the previous six months. On October 2, 2012, three weeks after the attacks, Darrell Issa (R-CA, chairman of the Committee) and Jason Chaffetz (R-UT, chairman of the subcommittee on National Security, Homeland Defense, and Foreign Operations) sent a letter to Secretary of State Clinton, which listed a number of these events—including car-jacking, kidnappings, assassination attempts, and gun battles. The letter stated, "Put together, these events indicated a clear pattern of security threats that could only be reasonably interpreted to justify increased security for US personnel and facilities in Benghazi.

In May 2012 an Al-Qaeda affiliate calling itself the Imprisoned Omar Ahmar Rahman Brigades claimed responsibility for an attack on the International Red Cross (ICRC) office in Benghazi. On August 6th the ICRC suspended operations in Benghazi. The head of the ICRC's delegation in Libya said the aid group was "appalled" by the attack and "extremely concerned" about escalating violence in Libya.

In early September 2012, Chris went out for a run in Tripoli when someone threw rocks at him. From then on security limited Chris to running in the grounds of the embassy compound.

A week before his murder in Benghazi, a State Department travel warning cited increasing assassinations, car bombs and gunmen abducting foreighners. "Clashes among militias can erupt at any time or any plae in the country," it cautioned.

Chapter 32

Murder in Benghazi

"When someone you love becomes a memory, the
memory becomes a treasure"

– Anonymous

It was 7am September 12, 2012, and I was at home
in Laguna Beach, California, drinking my morning
coffee in bed and watching the *Today Show.*

"This is NBC breaking news," said Matt Lauer.
"What started as scattered violence, then, escalating
violence against the American Embassy in Cairo and
the US Consulate in Benghazi, Libya, has taken on a
very deadly turn here."

A chill ran through my body. I stared at the
television unable to absorb the face I had just seen
flash across the screen. The man pictured had blond-
gray hair, blue eyes, and a big white grin that I knew so
well. His name was written on the screen right
underneath the picture but I wasn't wearing my
glasses. As I walked towards the television to a get
closer look, the image disappeared. Flames burned in
the background. I turned to face my boyfriend Michael
who was lying in bed next to me reading.

"Who were they talking about?" I asked.

Michael looked up from his iPad.

"The US embassy got attacked in Libya."

"Who is the man they were talking about, the one who was killed?"

Michael just stared at me.

I repeated my question more urgently.

"Chris Stevens. Why?"

I could feel my knees shaking and a sharp pain pierced my heart. My blurry vision worsened.

Oh God, I thought, what was going on? "He's the man I was engaged to." I said.

I was filled with shock and disbelief. I just wanted to run, to scream, but I couldn't. I wanted to throw up. I sat on the bed and kept staring at the TV screen. It couldn't be him. It had to be a mistake. There must be another Chris Stevens. Then his image reappeared on the screen. I grabbed my glasses and put them on; there was no mistake, it was Chris, my skinny chicken, gone forever.

Matt Lauer continued, "Reuters and AFP are reporting that the American ambassador to Libya has been killed in an attack on the US Consulate in Benghazi and also reporting that three other State Department workers have been killed, as well. What NBC can tell you, what we have confirmed, a Greek contractor with the US Mission in Benghazi is telling NBC that he identified the body of Ambassador Chris Stevens in a Benghazi street earlier today."

I stared at the TV set from far away, and for an instant, I saw myself in space looking down on Earth and everything on it a small speck in the overall scheme of things. My life would never be the same again. Chris was gone.

I made my way to the kitchen in a daze to make

smoothies, part of our usual routine, something predictable and normal which I desperately needed. I opened the fridge and got out the berries, celery, and Greek yogurt. My right hand, ready to dump some blueberries in the blender, started to shake. The blueberries spilled out onto the counter and I just stared at them while they rolled towards the edge. Frozen, I watched them tumble to the floor, one after another, scattering in all directions. The last one slid across the floor, hitting the baseboard. I gazed at that one small blueberry while tears cascaded down my cheeks.

Before Michael left for the office, he gave me a gentle hug. Until that day he had never heard me mention Chris. Michael knew that I had been engaged, but he did not know to whom. He could not imagine the depth of loss that I felt for Chris. As soon as Michael was out the door, I cried uncontrollably.

So many old friends who recognized Chris on the news and knew about our relationship called me that day. Yes, Chris was a great guy, and he didn't deserve to die. He was loved everywhere by so many people. How could this have happened to him in a country he fought so hard to help liberate? I spoke by telephone with Taieb, who had been Chris's best friend in Egypt.

"You always had a special place in his heart, Lydie," Taieb said. "Yours and Chris's was one of the best love stories I ever witnessed, true love."

Ironically, my boyfriend Michael never had to deal with Chris when he was alive, but now that Chris was dead, his ghost was suddenly a strong presence in the room with us. After a long day of seeing patients and being in the OR, Michael, an ear, nose, throat physician, would come home wanting to enjoy a nice quiet dinner and to watch the news. But after days of witnessing my pain over the continuous headlines about Benghazi, Michael switched over to watching the Travel Channel. When I became more and more possessed by the need to make sense of Chris's tragic end, Michael was alternately supportive and irritated as I was pulled further into reliving my past.

It soon became clear to me that entire volumes of Chris's story were being overlooked. As corny and overused as this may sound, Chris Stevens was a genuine American hero. He was the first American on the ground in Tripoli when the United States re-established diplomatic relations with General Gaddafi in 2002, and he was the first American on the ground to meet with rebel leaders plotting to overthrow the despised dictator on April 5, 2011. Chris would have scorned the politicians for spending so much time looking for someone to blame for his murder even though justice was something he valued. Instead Chris would want to know who would lead next on the several initiatives he had put into action during the short time he had served as Ambassador to better the lives of the Libyan people.

Few know that Chris had been scheduled to attend a meeting at Benghazi Hospital on the morning of September 12, 2012. The meeting's agenda included discussing progress on an ambitious project he was spearheading for a new division of emergency medicine, one of several initiatives he had undertaken to better the lives of the Libyan people since becoming ambassador just months before. Ironically, his physical presence for the meeting was tragically achieved when his bruised body was carried through the streets to the hospital.

Chapter 33

Tragedy Strikes

"I've learned that people will forget what you said,
people will forget what you did, but people will never
forget how you make them feel"

– Maya Angelou

On September 11th, 2012, in America, Gene Cretz, who preceded Chris as Ambassador to Libya, was sworn-in as the U.S. Ambassador to Ghana by Secretary of State Hillary Rodham Clinton. The same day that Chris was begging for security, Clinton was swearing in the former Ambassador to Libya as the new Ambassador to Ghana. Obviously Libya was on her mind.

Chris had traveled in Benghazi on a commercial flight the morning of September 10th, 2012. Traveling with him were two of the six Diplomatic Security Agents assigned to the Embassy in Tripoli. His trip had originally been scheduled for November 2012. But Secretary of State Hillary Clinton had personally asked him to take on the assignment to be the American physical presence in Benghazi for the anniversary of 9/11. The Benghazi Consulate also provided cover for the nearby covert CIA Annex that monitored local

Islamist militant operations. The most powerful of those local Islamist militant groups, Ansar al-Shariah, had more control over the Benghazi area than the Libyan government. This Islamist militia group advocated the implementation of strict Sharia Law across Libya.

At about 9:45PM, the Embassy in Tripoli received word of the attack in Benghazi. Gregory Hicks, second in rank at the Embassy, spoke via cell phone with Chris, who said, "We're under attack." Then the phone went dead. When Chris went missing, Hicks became the senior American diplomat in Libya for the remainder of the attack and its immediate aftermath. His words, therefore, are particularly authoritative.

Gregory Hicks quickly notified the State Department Operations Center in Washington and communicated with the CIA Annex in Benghazi. He then telephoned the Libyan government to request military help.

Frustrated by the locked metal bars, Ansar al-Shariah fighters doused the residence building where Chris was with diesel fuel and set it ablaze. I cannot imagine what was going through Chris's mind at the time. Was he frightened? Or did he have a way of concentrating only on the things he could control? We will never know.

Because Libyan militants had formed a protective perimeter around the residence, American security agents crawled through the burning building to attempt to rescue Chris and his Information Management Officer, Sean Smith. Smith was found dead, but Chris was nowhere in sight, presumed abducted. As the militants' perimeter collapsed, the American agents fled towards the CIA annex one mile away through a hail of gunfire and explosions.

We now know that Chris and Sean Smith had retreated into an impenetrable safe room. The attackers were unable to blast the door open, but smoke from the fire found its way into the tightly enclosed space. With no breathing apparatus, Chris and Sean died from smoke inhalation. But of course no one will ever know for certain what really took place except Chris and Sean. I have nightmares about that night, about Chris's rising panic as his whole life flashed before his eyes.

Chapter 34

Back to San Francisco, 2013

"I gain strength, courage and confidence by every experience in which I must stop and look fear in the face... I say to myself, I've loved through this and can take the next thing that comes along."

– Eleanor Roosevelt

One year after Chris's death, Michael and I traveled to the Bay Area to visit friends. I had been looking for an opportunity to drop in to see Chris's mother, Mary, and this was a perfect opportunity. While our friends had other plans, Michael and I drove to Piedmont where Mary and her husband Bob, Chris's stepdad lived. I hadn't seen Mary and Bob for quite some time and was nervous.

I was fidgeting on the morning of our visit. I had told Mary we would arrive at 12 noon, and didn't want to be late. I had an important question to ask Mary. We arrived on time. Bob, at 92 years old, hadn't changed a bit. He was still alert, and had the same warm twinkle in his eyes. Mary looked the same, too. She still wore her hair cut mid-length, healthy and thick, although now gray. Mary and I hugged immediately, then pulled back to look at each other. Her light blue eyes, the same color as Chris's, her first-born child, filled with emotion. A year had passed since she lost Chris, but I could see in her face that she didn't know how to even start to live again without him.

Bob, Mary, Michael and I sat on the little back patio. Mary poured each of us a small glass of sherry and set out some hors d'oeuvres. I was numb. I didn't know what to say.

Michael kept looking in my direction, hoping I would broach the subject of Chris. We soon moved to the dining area. In honor of my heritage, Bob had made French onion soup, a green salad, and dessert. Bob loved cooking. Mary, I remembered, was also a good cook.

After a while, Michael took the conversation reins himself, telling Bob and Mary about his background, that he was from Denmark, he was an ear, nose and throat doctor, and so on. An hour and a half passed before someone finally mentioned Chris. It was Bob. He spoke about various memorials and funds that the family was working on to honor Chris's legacy. For one, the family was helping to establish scholarships in Middle Eastern Studies at Chris's alma mater, the University of California, Berkeley. It was a very polite way to talk about Chris without touching on what really hurt.

After coffee, we gathered in the living room. Bob and Michael sat on one side of the room, while Mary and I sat together on a small loveseat on the other.

"I found a few pictures of the two of you in a box of Chris's belongings," said Mary. "I think you should have them."

She handed them to me, along with a small gift package wrapped in Egyptian hieroglyphic paper with a lavender bow neatly sealed on top. Inside I found a framed picture of Chris and me taken at the party where we first met in Cairo on September 11, 1994. Mary told me that Chris had always kept this photo on his home desk in Washington, DC, up until the day that he died. I felt a lump form inside my throat. I wanted to burst out weeping, but held back as much as I could, my eyes stinging with tears; so many memories, so many good times, now gone.

Mary took me into the kitchen and showed me a beautiful Middle Eastern piece of art hanging on the wall that Chris had bought for her in Jerusalem. On her fridge was a stick figure drawing of Chris, created by one of his young nieces, "I love my uncle Chris," was scrawled in crayon.

We returned to the living room and stopped by the piano. On top of it were numerous photos of Chris. There were some articles that Mary had kept for me. She showed me a heavy folder that contained every condolence letter written to her by political figures including President Obama and Secretary of State Clinton. Mary handed me the letter from the Secretary, and said, "She is very, very, very sorry."

Mary showed me photos of her daughter Anne and her son-in-law on their wedding day, as well as her son Tom and his wife on their wedding day. I realized how much Chris was like his mother, a nurturing, calming, and mature presence. Mary looked at me in a way that both of us understood; there was one set of photos and story missing in Mary's album, it was Chris's wedding photo.

When I told Mary I wanted to write a memoir about Chris and me, she immediately gave her blessing.

The process, she believed, would help me cope with the pain. But deep down I knew that the pain over Chris would always be there, gripping me like an iron fist that won't let go.

Chapter 35

My One-on-One with Gregory Hicks

"For us, the people that go out under the edge to represent our country, we believe that if we get in trouble, they're coming to get us, that our back is covered. To hear that it's not—that is a terrible, terrible experience."

– Gregory Hicks

On Wednesday, May 8, 2013, Gregory Hicks—Chris's deputy chief of mission (DCM) and right-hand man—delivered powerful testimony to Congress, revealing a detailed account of what happened in the final few hours after the terrorist attack. Hicks, a high level diplomat, holds a distinguished record of 25 years of service in six overseas assignments including Bahrain, Afghanistan, Libya, Yemen, Syria, and the Gambia. He has received six Meritorious Service Increases, three individual Meritorious Honor awards, and four individual Superior Honor awards. Hicks testified before Congress, that when he got the call Chris had been killed, it was "the saddest moment of my career." Currently Hicks is a State Department visiting fellow at the Center for

Strategic and International Studies.

On September 11, 2014, I read the news headline, and the attack at Benghazi had been omitted, no mention of Ambassador Chris Stevens or his life. I felt angrier than ever before. Chris and the heroic sacrifice he made for his country were becoming a distant memory. I decided to post a remembrance on Chris's Facebook page:

In loving memory to all whose lives were lost on September 11th, 2001... And let's not forget the Benghazi attack that killed 4 Americans on September 11th,

2012 including my friend and former fiancé, Ambassador Chris Stevens.

Two years have passed since the Benghazi tragedy, and the politicians in Washington continue to point fingers over who is to blame. Because Chris did not die in combat, the media has depicted him as a victim not a hero. But Chris Stevens was indeed a hero. He was the first American on the ground in Tripoli when the United States re-established diplomatic relations with General Muammar Gaddafi in 2002, and he was the first American on the ground to meet with rebel leaders plotting to overthrow the despised dictator on April 5, 2011. Throughout his diplomatic career Chris took risks that placed him in many such dangerous settings.

Chris would have scorned the politicians for spending so much time playing the blame game. Instead, he would have wanted to know who would carry out the initiatives he had put into action during his short tenure as ambassador. Chris's murder got the attention of the world, and the Benghazi attack remains a hot media topic that is once again making daily headlines. The story continues to revolve around politicians protecting themselves, yet Chris's contributions to his country have been forgotten.

In a CNN article, Jan Stevens, Chris's father said, "Chris was not willing to be the kind of diplomat who would strut around in fortified compounds. He amazed and impressed the Libyans by walking the streets with the lightest of escorts, sitting in sidewalk cafes, chatting with passers-by. There was a risk to being accessible. He knew it, and he accepted it."

His whole life, Chris was busy trying to represent America's most coveted democratic principles such as individual freedom and respect of human rights.

Shortly after creating this brief remembrance of Chris on Facebook, one of Chris's colleagues, Henry Bisharat, contacted me. Henry later put me in touch with Gregory Hicks and we communicated through social media. We hit it off immediately, and he agreed to speak with me at his home near Washington, D.C. A couple of months later, I was on a plane to Washington preparing to meet with Gregory who welcomed me warmly into his home in the suburbs outside of D.C. As soon as I arrived at his house he said, "We've met before!"

"We did? I feel really bad not remembering it!"

"Don't feel bad. It's a long time ago. It was 1997 and you came to my office with Chris at the State Department."

We then talked at length about Chris as well as the events that took place during the week Chris died.

"On the night of September 9, 2012, two nights

before his death, Chris was very downbeat. He said he was only going to stay in Libya for two years. It was just too tough. Chris was usually the optimistic one, but for once, I was the one who was upbeat about getting American companies back to Libya and opening a school. Chris had just returned to Libya from Sweden where he had a really good time. He told me, "I don't know what my future holds." "He also mentioned retiring."

Gregory Hicks was the Deputy Chief of Mission for Libya the night that Ambassador Chris Stevens died, and as Chris' number two man, he is a key witness to what occurred in Benghazi. Hicks, was the last person to speak with Chris Stevens before he died, and he has first-hand knowledge of the hundreds of requests that he and Chris made for more security in Benghazi. Anyone can count them; over six hundred requests were made for more personnel with guns to protect the Ambassador and his staff so that they could carry out their mission in Benghazi. All were ignored.

On September 10, 2012, Chris traveled to Benghazi. He was doing advance work for a trip to Benghazi planned by Secretary Clinton for October. His previously planned trip in August had been cancelled because of security concerns. The Benghazi "consulate" also provided cover for the nearby covert CIA 'annex' that monitored local Islamist militant operations. The most powerful of those local Islamist militant groups, Ansar al-Shariah, had more control over the Benghazi area than the Libyan government.

Greg went on to describe what happened from his perspective on September 11, 2012: "After breakfast, I sent a few emails to American companies who were onboard as financiers to open a school in Benghazi the following year. I watched on TV the events unfolding in Cairo and texted Chris, "Are you paying attention to what's going on in Cairo?" Chris texted back, "What is going on?" And I told him, "The embassy is being stormed." "I know that Chris watched TV all that afternoon in Benghazi to monitor the riots in Egypt."

Greg Hicks confirmed that no one reported similar crowds forming in Egypt. "In Tripoli," he continued, "we were all very tense that day. We were very worried about ourselves in Tripoli. So we minimized movement. We pretty much stayed put that day, not doing much. And we could not have outside appointments or anything like that. About 9 pm the sun was down and I felt a sigh of relief that it was night and we could be relatively confident that nothing was going to happen. We were through with the day. And I started to watch some TV and unwind and this is when it all started in Benghazi."

At about 9:45PM, Greg Hicks received a call via cell phone from a number he didn't know. He had missed the call. When he listened to the message, it was Chris who had borrowed the phone from one of the DS agents to call Gregory, "We're under attack." Then the phone went dead.

Hicks quickly notified the State Department Operations Center in Washington and communicated with the CIA Annex in Benghazi. He then telephoned the Libyan government to request military help.

"The next day, on the 12th, we evacuated the compound," said Hicks. "We each took one bag and were gone. We left everything there and the Libyans to guard it. Until we were in the sky, and we were far away from Libya, we had no idea if we would make it out alive. I am in such great admiration of the American security operators and other CIA guys [Diplomatic Security Service operators] from the Annex, who were there to help provide security in Benghazi. The way that they conducted themselves is truly in the spirit of America.

I compare the assault on Benghazi and the way these guys behaved to the battle of Mobile Bay, which took place in 1864 during the Civil War when the US Navy was trying to sail into the harbor. They were getting fired at. And, of course, at the time it was wooden ships, and they had to sail the sailboat in between two forts and the enemy had put mines in the passageway. Back then mines were called torpedoes. So they were being bombarded and they were fighting back also and one of the sailors said to the admiral, 'Sir there are torpedoes in the channel.'

"And the admiral answered, Damn the torpedoes! Full speed ahead!"

"And they sailed between the forts. Once they were in the harbor, they only lost one ship and they captured the city. And in the case of the security guys in Benghazi they did just that. And because of that, 30 people are alive today. Because at one point one of the security operators said, "Damn what they want, full speed ahead."

If you want to watch a reenactment of the attack in Benghazi, I recommend the film and the book *Thirteen Hours,* both of which do a good job of portraying the heroism of the DSAs realistically.

Three weeks before he died, Chris and I

exchanged emails. I signed off with these words "Stay away from bullets." My last words to the man I once believed would be the father of my children.

Chapter 36

Telling the Truth

"Before you speak, ask yourself, is it kind, is it necessary, is it true, does it improve on the silence?"

– Sai Baba

When a person you love dies, you want to know why. At least I do. Often, it is easy to know the answer. Someone who dies of cancer in the hospital receives a death certificate stating the disease. A soldier killed in the line of duty receives a posthumous commendation explaining the circumstances of his death, and a mother who dies during childbirth has this written up in her medical records before being sent to the morgue.

When Chris Stevens died, I wanted to know why, when, how. I did not try to assess blame; I needed the answers to process my grief. Many people who have lost loved ones will understand this. I suppose that is one reason why we have accountability for death caused by criminal intent. When a loved one is the victim of a hit-and-run driver the authorities and public do everything to locate the killer and provide other details about what occurred. But when a U.S. Ambassador was murdered in a remote city in the Middle East, the President did not allow that to upset his plans, instead, he flew from

Washington to Las Vegas the next day for a fundraiser. We should not be surprised then that no one has been helpful at getting to the truth about what happened to Chris Stevens and why.

In the days immediately following the attack, US National Security Advisor Susan Rice, who was then serving as the Ambassador to the United Nations, appeared on national television multiple times to reinforce the position that the deadly violence in Benghazi was the result of protests and an anti-Muslim video, "The Innocents of Muslims."

In one of the interviews for Fox News Sunday, Rice said: "Based on the best information we have to date, what our assessment is at present is in fact what began spontaneously in Benghazi as a reaction to what had transpired some hours earlier in Cairo where, of course, as you know, there was a violent protest outside of our embassy, sparked by this hateful video. But soon after that spontaneous protest began outside of our consulate in Benghazi, we believe that it looks like extremist elements, individuals, joined in that...in that effort with heavy weapons of the sort that are, unfortunately, readily now available in Libya post-revolution. And that it had spun from there into something much, much more violent." "We do not—we do not have information at present that leads us to conclude that this was premeditated or preplanned. I think it's clear that there were extremist elements that joined in and escalated the violence. Whether they were Al Qaeda affiliates, whether they were Libyan-based extremists or Al Qaeda itself I think is one of the things we'll have to determine."

Although Secretary Rice took most of the heat as

the designated face of the Administration, Secretary of State Hillary Clinton was in charge of the compound at Benghazi and was Chris's boss. So it is significant that Rice's repeated appearances reinforced the following statement made by Clinton at 10:08 pm EST, while the attack was still going on: "Some have sought to justify the vicious behavior as a response to inflammatory material posted on the internet." Under questioning by Congress, Secretary Clinton tried to emphasize the ambiguous words in this statement, but she never explained why she did not call a halt to Secretary Rice's forceful and repeated reinforcement of her original explanation of what had occurred when she knew that it was simply false.

During nearly two years following the attack, Secretary Clinton testified under oath to both houses of Congress without revealing that she was sitting on piles of emails that were relevant to Benghazi, because she had conducted all her email correspondence on a private server, not on the usual State Department server as required by every spy service in the federal government. After her private server was discovered almost by accident by a hacker, and long legal battles forced production of the emails, it was learned that within the same hour Secretary Clinton released her public statement blaming the "inflammatory material posted on the internet," she reported to her family that "two officers were killed today in Benghazi by an Al Qaeda-like group."

During frustrating research to discover the truth, most of us noticed early on that Rice's account was directly contradicted by that of Libyan President Mohamed Yousef El-Magariaf, who said that he had "no doubt" the attack was pre-planned by individuals from outside Libya. As it turned out, this was evident when Secretary Clinton told him, "Ansar al-Sharia is claiming responsibility." So once again, Secretary Clinton blamed a terrorist group, not protesters.

I did not go through these details to choose sides in the political debate, which rages on as I write these lines. I only point out that no one seems interested in digging for the facts to learn the truth about what happened to Ambassador Chris Stevens, Sean Smith, Tyrone Woods and Glen Doherty who died tragically and needlessly that day. Instead, they either want to obscure the truth to protect a political position or learn enough to bring down an opponent. Neither is true to the American spirit of pursuing truth for its own sake.

Chapter 37

Lies

"A single lie destroys a whole reputation of integrity"

– Baltasar Gracian

I have attempted to share as much as I know about Chris Stevens, the man, with you the reader. My interest was never political. In my quest for the facts, I discovered only one man I could trust to speak the truth, Gregory Hicks. After the State Department confiscated all the relevant evidence he once possessed, ultimately locking him out of the building where he once worked, I decided to make a small contribution to shining a light on the Benghazi investigation, by publishing some of my conversation with him. Gregory has provided such clarity for me as I sort through my personal history with Chris and I didn't want to take a chance on leaving anything out that may be of importance or to dispel myths and deliberate falsehoods that often appear in any high profile tragedy, particularly those connected to growing government scandals.

Political blogs are notorious for taking one false minute item and blowing it so out of proportion that it is accepted as fact when it is not. A disturbing example of this happened soon after Chris's murder. It was in such bad taste that I considered not mentioning it at all. With apologies to anyone who identifies as LGBT and who may be offended, I must be clear that it is out of love and respect for both Chris and the truth that I need to dispel a rumor that is complete nonsense but useful to those who are masters of diversion and spin.

Chris's best friend in high school, Austin Tichenor, posted a photograph of the two of them on Facebook after Chris died. Some people, who were not thinking of the long term implications, conjured a lie that they were gay lovers based on stereotypes of brightly colored clothing and the fact that Chris had never been married. Then the politicians jumped into the fray, fanning the flames of bigotry and using them to blame the victim: since Muslims dislike gay behavior, they said, Chris's supposed sexual preference must have set off the attack.

For those of us who knew Chris, nothing could be more ridiculous. The attack, of course, was about power since Libyans had been engaged in a volatile battle for it from the moment Gaddafi was overthrown. The photo of the supposedly gay lovers had originally been taken with four people, Chris and Austin with their two dates. Austin's date was his high school/college sweetheart, and Jan was Chris's date. Austin's wife, Dee, the mother of his two children, suggested he crop the girls out of the picture, after all she wasn't in Austin's life at the time. This cropped picture was the root of the rumor that Chris was gay. I've never been married and I've never had children but this doesn't mean I am gay. The double standard was in effect and like a snowball rolling downhill it just grew bigger although it was totally baseless.

As for the inappropriate question about whether a dead man was gay, I, of course will vouch for his heterosexuality. Chris definitely was attracted to women. My close friend and hairdresser Terry, who is part of the gay community found this story ludicrous. He and I have been best friends for over twenty years, "definitely not gay", he said, having met Chris when we were together. An open secret within the State Department family is that Chris was known, as the Warren Beatty of the diplomatic core.

Also circulating was the story that Chris had met with Ali Akin, the Turkish consul general in Benghazi, earlier on the night that Chris had been killed. Gossip in the media had it that Akin was Chris's lover in Libya. According to Gregory Hicks, Chris's second in command in Libya, this was absolutely a lie. Chris's meeting with the Turkish diplomat revolved around confidential political issues.

As his former fiancée and close friend, I was so dismayed that entire volumes of Chris's life story were being buried along with him except for the gossip about his sexuality. The gay rumor was rooted in the fact that he had remained unmarried after our engagement and it was a perfect opportunity to divert the public's attention away from the real cause of his death in Benghazi.

When I interviewed Gregory Hicks for this book, we both had to share a laugh over the gay rumor. Greg told me, "Chris was someone who floated from one woman to another." Indeed. Chris had many girlfriends before he and I were engaged and many thereafter.

Chris's Perugia friend Wijffels also remembers that everyone, especially women, were drawn to Chris's aura "Chris represented to me the epitome of the American success formula: athletic, handsome, smart, polite, funny, resilient, light-hearted and broadly smiling," said Wijffels.

While Chris had a reputation as a ladies man, he and I shared a monogamous relationship. During that time, I held onto the hope that we would be together forever, but looking back now, I have to admit to myself that he always maintained a distance. Perhaps this is because it was not easy for him to combine family and life as a diplomat. I remember Chris being obsessed with the Egyptian Nobel Prize-winning writer Naguib Mahfouz and his novel *Respected Sir*, about a poor civil servant whose sole goal in life is to rise to the position of Director General of his department, and be addressed as "Respected Sir", passing up love, marriage, and family along the way. He achieves his goal, finally, but at great personal sacrifice.

Chapter 38

Aftermath: September 2012 – February 2015

"A friend who dies, it's something of you who dies"

– Gustave Flaubert

So many lies were told after Chris died that I thought I would never learn the truth. At first, US National Security Advisor Susan Rice, who was then serving as the Ambassador to the United Nations, appeared on the national news networks to reinforce the story that the deadly violence in Benghazi had resulted from protests against an anti-Muslim video, "The Innocents of Muslims." The producer of that video was arrested and his imprisonment publicized to show that America does not tolerate such acts.

Secretary of State Hillary Clinton, who was Chris's boss, also issued a statement a few minutes after 10 p.m., while the assault was still occurring, which Secretary Rice's video story reinforced: "Some have sought to justify the vicious behavior as a response to inflammatory material posted on the internet." Later, the government conceded that there were no riots in Benghazi, only in Egypt, and the killing was, in fact, premeditated murder by a terrorist organization.

In October, 2012, Secretary Clinton, told CNN, "I take responsibility" for what occurred, but she diluted it with a clever trick. She said, "I'm in charge of the State Department's sixty thousand-plus people all over the world, two hundred and seventy five posts." This made me believe that Chris was just one of her many Ambassadors and that her level of knowledge about what occurred was equivalent to only 1/275th of the attention she was able to give Libya. I was naïve to the world of politician-speak and did not know this was only a form of deception; when a politician actually knows something and says, in effect, she does not, that is a lie.

In October, 2012, information about a lack of security in Benghazi also began to leak out to the public. Eric Nordstrom held the post of Regional Security Officer (RSO) for the area that covered Libya, which means he was in charge of providing security for the Foreign Service mission in Benghazi. When I first learned about this, I wondered whether Nordstrom was the person most responsible for Chris's death. After all, why didn't security personnel protect Chris against the attack?

In the aftermath of the Benghazi attack, Nordstrom told investigators that he had tried to get more armed security guards assigned to Benghazi, but persons in the State Department had rejected his efforts. The "assets" used for security in Tripoli and Benghazi were civilians recruited from the Navy Seals or other elite military units. These individuals were capable of generating significant firepower, which allowed the United States to assign a relatively few to protect diplomats in remote locations like Benghazi. RSO Nordstrom had asked that twelve of these security guards be assigned full time to Benghazi. That request was refused; only three of these assets were assigned to Benghazi on September 11, 2012. Six, however, were assigned to Tripoli, and Ambassador Stevens brought two of these fighting assets with him as his personal bodyguards when he traveled to Benghazi on September 10. So there were a total of five security personnel available to hold off a virtual army of terrorist fighters when the attack came at about 9:45 p.m. on September 11, 2012.

The individuals who refused RSO Nordstrom's request for additional security in Benghazi were under Secretary of State for Management Patrick Kennedy, who reported directly to Hillary Clinton, and Deputy Assistant Secretary of State for International Programs Charlene Lamb. In testimony before a Congressional committee in October, 2012, Kennedy and Lamb defended their decision.

"We regularly assess risk and resource allocation," Kennedy testified in October, 2012, "a process involving the considered judgments of experienced professionals on the ground and in Washington, using the best available information." Ms. Lamb testified only that the State Department "had the correct number of assets in Benghazi at the time."

Who, exactly, were the "experienced professionals" who made the "considered judgments" that additional "assets" were not needed in Benghazi, and what facts did they rely on to form those judgments? Obviously, Mr. Nordstrom was not among them. It would take me more than three years to find the answers to these questions, and by that time, Ms. Lamb had placed all of the blame for inadequate security on Mr. Nordstrom and the victim, Ambassador, Chris Stevens.

The most egregious lie told in the immediate aftermath of the Benghazi attack was the one not spoken. From the date of Chris's murder until she was caught in March, 2015, Hillary Clinton concealed from the American people, including those who loved him, that on a private server at home she had over 30,000 pages of emails that covered subjects involving Benghazi.

During those thirty months, I had grown frustrated from the challenge of facing so many gaps in the story presented by the media as well as the seven reports published by various committees and task forces. So it was a relief and a revelation to learn that there was a logical explanation for those gaps. I wasn't crazy after all.

Many new details soon surfaced. For example, an email was provided from Mrs. Clinton's private server in which she sent a note to her family at 11:00 pm Eastern time that stated: "two officers were killed today in Benghazi by an Al Qaeda-like group," not by protesters angry about a video as had been reported initially. She sent this email less than an hour after issuing her public statement suggesting that blame should fall on "inflammatory material posted on the internet." It was also learned through other records a call she made to the Egyptian Prime Minister that night stating, "We know the attack in Libya had nothing to do with the film. It was a planned attack, not a protest."

She sent the email to her family confirming a

terrorist attack less than an hour after her statement to the public that "Some have sought to justify the vicious behavior as a response to inflammatory material posted on the internet." With her lawyer's hat on, she might parse words and say that the memo sent to the public does not state definitively what brought on the attack, but the lie is in the suggestion of what might be compared to her absolute knowledge of what was. I am not a lawyer and do not care whether Hillary Clinton is guilty of a criminal wrong; I only care that she concealed from the public and those grieving for Chris so much vital information for thirty months when she had a moral duty to reveal it earlier.

Chapter 39

Libya Then and Now

"You Bedouin of Libya, who saved our lives, though you
will dwell forever in my memory, yet I shall never be
able to recapture your features. You are Humanity and
your face comes into my mind simply as man incarnate.
You, our beloved fellowman, did not know who we
might be, and yet you recognized us without fail. And I,
in my turn, shall recognize you in the faces of mankind.
You came towards me in an aureole of charity and
magnanimity bearing the gift of water. All my friends
and all my enemies marched towards me in your
person. It did not seem to me that you were rescuing
me: rather did it seem that you were forgiving me. And I
felt I had no enemy left in all the world."

– Antoine De Saint-Exupery

In a September 13, 2012 New York Times OpEd,
"What Libya Lost," by Ethan Chorin, author of *Exit
the Colonel: The Hidden History of the Libyan
Revolution,* and a co-founder of the Avicenna Group, a
nonprofit organization working on Libya's medical
facilities, detailed how he was supposed to attend a
meeting on September 12, 2012 with Chris and others.
They were to discuss a plan for a new division of
emergency medicine at Benghazi Medical Center, the

largest modern hospital in eastern Libya. Chris was killed the night before and the meeting never took place.

"The draft agreement we were working on was the kind of visionary effort to improve life in Libya that Ambassador Stevens liked—in this case, a collaboration between doctors in Boston and Benghazi, brokered by a nongovernmental organization that a Libyan-American and I had organized after the recent revolution," wrote Chorin. "Our goal was a center that could also serve as a training facility for all of eastern Libya. It was the kind of public-private and Libyan-American partnership that Ambassador Stevens believed could help Libya move beyond decades of stagnation and despotism."

Earlier on the night on September 10, 2012, Chris had told Chorin and the others by phone how happy he was that the project was nearing fruition. He emphasized how important it was to show the US government's support for initiatives like this. They made plans to meet with the medical center's director general, Dr. Fathi al-Jehani, at the hospital the next morning. Chorin noted that Dr. Jehani had also been a target of violence for his "forward-thinking views."

Chorin called Chris's security detail about a half an hour later to discuss the visit. "We've got a problem here," he said, and then the line went dead.

When Chorin and his colleagues returned to the medical center the morning after the attack, the Libyan doctor and other ER staffers who had tried to save Chris broke down in tears.

Chris's death caused a major setback for Benghazi, as well as the potential for increased instability in eastern Libya. Still, Chorin believes Libya is "still far better off today than it was under Qaddafi," particularly with the good relations Chris established with them on behalf of the United States government.

Today Libya's government is struggling to maintain order and rebuild state institutions amid rising violence since the ouster and subsequent death of Colonel Muammar al-Gaddafi in October 2011. The presence of rebel militias has increased approximately 1,700 armed groups especially since the attack on the U.S. consulate in Benghazi on September 11, 2012, and at least two hundred people have been killed in violent clashes and attacks in 2014 alone.

Following the June 2014 parliamentary elections, the House of Representatives (HoR) was elected to replace the General National Congress (GNC), which came to power in August 2012 after the first elections in a post-Gaddafi Libya. However, the HoR has struggled to consolidate legitimacy as the main authoritative power in Libya. Prime Minister Abdullah al-Thanay has tried to regain control of the government, but continues to face opposition from multiple fronts.

A former Gaddafi loyalist, retired General Khalifa Haftar began "Operation Dignity" in February 2014 with an initial focus on attacking Islamist militant groups in Benghazi. The movement gained momentum in May 2014 when Haftar called for the dissolution of the GNC. Counter to this revolutionary movement, an alliance of Islamists and militias formed "Operation Dawn" and seized the airport in Tripoli in August 2014. In late August 2014, the United Arab Emirates launched airstrikes from Egypt against Qatari-backed Islamist militias in Libya, but the strikes failed to prevent the militias from capturing the airport.

Previously, in July 2014, the Libyan government reached a deal with rebels to reopen two major oil ports in the country, resolving the country's oil crisis. Libya's government, however, remains fractured with rival militias envying for power in the western and eastern parts of the country. The United States, France, and the UK have also closed their embassies, and the UN withdrew its staff from Tripoli. In order to help rebuild and refocus Libya's security infrastructure, the United States will train 5,000 to 8,000 security forces as it is increasingly concerned about the prevalence of terrorist groups and potential weapons transfers across the country's unmonitored borders.

Due to the political turmoil and unrest, the US evacuated all staff from the embassy in Tripoli in July 2014. Today the US embassy to Libya sits on the island of Malta.

All so senseless, so inane, so ignorant, and it was all based on fear which was generated by hate for Americans with factions of Sunnis, Shiites, Russians, Americans, Turks, Saudis, Qataris and Iranians, all trying to get a piece of the new Libya pie. Libya was an axis of a Middle East that had gone insane.

Chris was caught right in the middle of the Arab Spring, a revolutionary wave of demonstrations and protests (violent and non-violent), riots, and civil wars in the Arab world that began on December 18, 2010. It was a blazing vat of boiling human emotions in Libya, and Chris was directly in the mezzo of it all working to raise awareness for Libyans on how to elevate their lives, to take their lives to a higher level with courses of action he was implementing to do so, and it cost him his life.

By the time Chris slipped into Benghazi off of that Greek ship in April 2011, he was already regarded as a knowledgeable hand among diplomats when it came to Libya. Chris knew the turf and the terrain. He understood people, the demographics and the tribal politics. He knew the importance of humanitarian aid and that speed mattered – being the first responder to the needs of the Libyan people was going to pay big dividends during the campaign. Chris did complete his mission and mandate as evidenced by the ousting of Gaddafi.

Chapter 40

Over The Edge

"No matter what anybody says about grief and about time healing wounds, the truth is, there are certain sorrows that never fade away until the heart stop beating and the last breath is taken."

– Anonymous

As the two-year anniversary of Benghazi rolled around on September 11, 2014, my sorrow gave way to more and more anger. The public, the media, and worst of all, the State Department seemed to be blaming Chris for his own fate. I realized that the story I needed to tell was so much bigger than the story of Chris and me. I needed to tell the personal story of J. Christopher Stevens, a career United States diplomat who had devoted his life to bettering the lives of the people in the Middle East, only to end up another casualty in a region that has spun out of control since he began his first tour there in the early 90's.

Chris was a leading expert on diplomacy in the Middle East, having spent most of his career there and in North Africa, holding posts in Israel, Egypt, Syria, and Saudi Arabia. He also served as Deputy Chief of Mission in Tripoli, Libya from 2007 to 2009, during the rule of Muammar Gaddafi, and served as the U.S.

Representative to the Libyan Transitional National Council in Benghazi, Libya from April to December 2011 before being appointed ambassador to Libya in 2012.

Chris's death raises serious questions about the US government's role in the Middle East and what we are trying to accomplish there. Are we really trying to help foster democracy or simply working to further US business interests? The world needs to know how American diplomats such as Chris don't make headlines until something horrible happens, and then it is the policy and politics that get attention.

In my quest to honor Chris's legacy it was inevitable that I also come face-to-face with the controversy surrounding what really happened in Benghazi. The tragic attack that took Chris's life is now almost four years behind us, yet the politicking continues. Many colleagues and friends of Chris, including Gregory Hicks, former deputy chief of mission in Libya, Chris's second in command, have broken their silence and come forward, wanting to help me fill in the blanks surrounding Chris's career history, including exactly what occurred on that horrific night in Benghazi.

Growing tired of hearing about the blame for lack of security being placed on Chris, Gregory Hicks tried to set the record straight in a Wall Street Journal editorial, published on January 22, 2014. In this opinion piece, Hicks states, "Chris Stevens was not responsible for the reduction in security personnel. His requests for additional security were denied or ignored. Officials at the State and Defense departments in Washington made the decisions that resulted in reduced security.

Senator Lindsey Graham stated on the Senate floor last week that Chris "was in Benghazi because that is where he was supposed to be doing what America wanted him to do: Try to hold Libya together." He added, "Quit blaming the dead guy."

During our years together, I can remember Chris writing religiously in his journal every night. It is public knowledge that Chris had been keeping a diary during his ambassadorship. Copies made of several loose diary pages, were somehow obtained by CNN several days following the attack. These pages revealed that he had been worried about security threats in Benghazi and the rise in Islamic extremism. This is also corroborated in the New York Times best seller '13 Hours: The inside Account of what Really Happened In Benghazi,' written by Mitchell Zuckoff. The security team members were posted at the Annex, the CIA station in Benghazi situated near the US Special Mission Compound, where the attack took place. Zuckoff's book details how the annex security team, comprised of six American operators, fought to avert the tragedy that took place, and succeeded in preventing tragedy on a much greater scale. Their account backs up Hicks's claim that the overall security in Benghazi was seriously wanting.

Chris rented a storage facility near his DC home in Chevy Chase, Maryland. Were all the diaries he wrote every year in there? If yes, what happened to them? It is believed, that if the State Department entered his storage and found his diaries, then those diaries have become the State Department's properties. Those diaries were most likely destroyed by the State Department. The diary Chris kept in Libya in 2012 was discovered in the fire wreckage in Benghazi and sent to

Tripoli. Shortly thereafter, the State Department ordered that it be handed over to Under Secretary of State Patrick Kennedy, second in command to Secretary of State Hillary Clinton.

If Chris had survived, I am certain that one day he would have written his own story. Since he is not here, I am compelled to tell the world not only about the precious years that I spent with him, but also about the road he took to achieve his lifelong dream of becoming a US ambassador, a dream lived out for only four short months before thwarted by tragedy.

Chapter 41

Remembering Chris Stevens

"Memories of our lives, of our works and our deed will continue in others."

– Rosa Parks

Shortly after Chris's passing, his family established the J. Christopher Stevens Fund. The fund's aim is to promote intercultural understanding between Americans and the people of the Middle East and will support educational programs, including student exchanges, libraries and the Peace Corps. The mission of the fund is to support activities that build bridges between the people of the United States and those of the broader Middle East, the mission to which Chris dedicated his life.

The Center for Middle Eastern Studies at the University of California, Berkeley, where Chris studied as an undergraduate, has also created the Ambassador J. Christopher Stevens Memorial Fund for Middle Eastern Studies, endowed by the J. Christopher Stevens Fund. The purpose is to encourage and inspire students in Middle Eastern and North African scholarship.

UC Berkeley with a coalition of public and private partners has also launched the J. Christopher

Stevens Virtual Exchange Initiative. This initiative will embrace the power of technology to fuel the largest ever increase in people-to-people exchanges between the United States and the broader Middle East, vastly increasing the number and diversity of youth who have a meaningful cross-cultural experience as part of their formative education, and reaching *over one million youth by 2020.*

On September 11, 2013, the Piedmont Unified District Board of Education voted to name the Piedmont High School Library the Ambassador J. Christopher Stevens Memorial Library.

Chris's sister Anne Stevens, a physician, has committed to carrying out the work her brother started on a program to expand medical care in Benghazi. Anne invited me to become involved in a Wired International global health education initiative which the J. Christopher Stevens Fund has helped support. On October 9, 2015, I joined Anne at Wired International's fundraiser for this project, which honors Chris and involves Berkeley graduate students traveling abroad to provide health and medical training in Africa, Latin America and Central Asia. It is a way to honor Chris's memory and carry forward the work that he cared for so deeply.

Chapter 42

Memories

"True love, especially first love, can be so tumultuous
and passionate that it feels like a violent journey."

– Holliday Grainger

W hen I was a little girl growing up in the
coastal area of Northern France, I held
Americans in high esteem. There were
reminders everywhere of the heroes who had come to
liberate France from the German invaders in 1944, not
just memorials where the names of men long dead are
carved and wreaths are laid but bunkers and tank
entrapments where men fought and died for the
freedom of our ancestors.

Though I had not been born yet when fighting
took place in my village in Brittany near the famous
beaches of Normandy, the history was taught that the
Americans were remarkable because unlike others who
had come to French shores with a mighty army, in this
case the mightiest army ever assembled, the Americans
came not to conquer but to heal; they brought only the
war materials they needed to rid our land of the tyrant,
though surely they were capable of making more, and
then left us with our freedom. Before they left, they gave
us wealth, the Marshall Plan so that we could rebuild

our country. And though we had no army that had earned it, the Americans gave us an equal seat at the table in the Security Council at the UN. All of this was unprecedented in history, and it is an ideal that many of us still hold.

Chris still lived that ideal every day. He recognized that many people in other countries believed that America had only come to take what they had, but he knew they were wrong. Chris optimistically believed he could find a way to communicate with those who were hostile so they would begin to trust him and understand through him, good intentions.

Chris Stevens was the bravest man I ever knew. I cannot imagine him ever "leading from behind". Chris always wanted to be the first boots on the ground. In Libya, he led the way into Tripoli when the George W. Bush administration recognized the Gaddafi regime, and then he was the first U.S. envoy into Benghazi in April 2011 when he sneaked ashore to join rebel leadership to help coordinate the fight to topple the Gaddafi regime; and then only a few months before his murder, Chris was named the first Ambassador to Libya in almost two years. Chris represented the American ideal that I had believed as a little girl that all Americans shared with the brave soldiers at Normandy; he came to Benghazi to help, not to conquer, heedless of the risk to himself. Such men are heroes, but they need looking after or they are sure to perish; it is not in their nature to look after themselves. They don't stand a chance without leaders who share their values.

In a SOFREP, a US and Coalition Military Special Operations Situation Report excerpt from Chris's last 3 days of his life, September 9, 2012, Chris noted,

"Stressful day. Too many things going on everyone wants to bend my ear. Need to pull above the fray."

Chris, as predictable as he was, still flickered with uncertainty and you just never knew exactly in what it would result. Birth, in the form of moisture, death in the form of black ice and as with Chris, although I was aware of the dangers of his work, I never once thought he would not make it to his sixtieth birthday. Was his notation a transparent statement, a knowledge and fear of the future he would never live to see?

"Do you remember the dreadful drive to Saqqara and we almost ran over the man?" Chris wrote to me, "A road that goes on forever. No lights, very hard to see." I certainly did.

Saqqara is a vast, ancient burial ground in Egypt. It serves as the necropolis (a large ancient cemetery with elaborate tomb monuments) for the Ancient Egyptian capital, Memphis. Like the Tule fog that gathers in the part of California where Chris was born, the mist sits right on the road, a blanket that covers everything like a death shroud. It blinds one's ability to see. Visibility is less than 500 feet. With black ice, one cannot stop in time to avoid a collision with another car, or with a human being. And it has resulted in many traffic fatalities.

Although I was never that consciously aware of it, after his death, it occurred to me that he may have been transmitting a premonition about his mortality, I don't know for sure if this is so, but he certainly gave hints of that throughout the time I knew him. And like the Tule fog, it comes as a surprise, like death.

His ambivalence about spending ten years in the

middle ranks of the Foreign Service made me consider again, his uncertainty, about his future. What to do? It was a constant concern that appeared to stalk Chris throughout my time with him.

Now, again, after Chris's horrifying death and how he was left alone without any protection, I am haunted by what he wrote. How alone did he feel at the end when he was fighting his way through the smoke-filled consulate rooms to find some air to breathe?

I well imagine what was going through his mind during the last moments of his life and believe he was desperately trying to save himself. But for Chris or the other men to be put in this position is unacceptable. For the government that Chris relied on to shirk the protection of a United States Ambassador because of budget restrictions is unfathomable. Deadly corners were cut so that billions of dollars in taxpayer money could be funneled out to other countries. How can that be? What sort of skewed logic would implement a plan that trades money for human lives? It all boils down to the cold hearted business of politics, a game that is played despite the deadly consequences for those caught in the middle, defenseless and unaware.

EPILOGUE

"When one door of happiness closes, another opens;
but often we look so long at the closed door that we do
not see the one which has opened for us"

– Helen Keller

In an email dated September 13th, 2014, Chris's mother
Mary wrote:

Lydie dear,

*Merci beaucoup for the huge and gorgeous
bouquet that was delivered to our door on the morning of
the 11th. You are such a dear to remember and to send
it. I am attaching here a picture of it on our piano
alongside of a nice picture of Chris (taken I don't
remember when). Also there by the flowers is the bronze
medal of a mythical man meant to represent Chris
connecting two worlds with a bridge, uncompleted. It
was made by a friend, a woman who was a Hungarian
refugee to the US in the 1950s. She, Marika Somogyi is
now a well-known sculptor, especially of bronze
commemorative medals. She has given us permission to
give it as an award to anyone or group we feel deserve
it. And next to that is the crystal figure of the world that
was awarded posthumously to Chris last year by a U.S.
national committee on conciliation and non-violence. We
went to their Minneapolis conference to accept the award
for him. I put our flag out on the deck for the week, and*

we have received many kind wishes and memories from many friends and relatives. It's a good support. A friend in Grass Valley reports that Chris's grave has many bouquets on it this week, so he is remembered up there, too. I admire you for getting going on writing down your memories; you have already had an extraordinarily interesting life—and you are not even half through it! We do hope to see you sometime soon. Robert joins me in sending love,

Mary

Please stop to consider what an extraordinary man Chris was. He still held high the American ideal, and he had perfected his extraordinary empathy so that people would trust him enough to listen to this message. Chris Stevens was the bravest man I ever met; his courage allowed him to take reasonable risks when required by his mission, and because of that he could always be counted on reliably to keep his word—to carry out his mission even when it was risky.

When Chris and I finally decided to part ways, I knew that he was committed to becoming an ambassador more than anything else, and that this was his destiny. At one time he wanted a family, but in the end, his desire to change the world superseded everything else. Like so many people in history who have left a lasting mark, Chris was not interested in living a normal, peaceful, safe, and secure existence. There was something far more compelling that he had to pursue and catch before his time tragically ran out.

Before Chris died, I was content with my life; interested in everything, an active traveler, but not too interested in politics. I did not care too much, really, who would become our next president, and it was all the same to me, I thought if politicians told fibs to keep their jobs. I care more about politics now because I have seen what happens when our elected officials do not behave well and when they are not held accountable for their actions. Only now have I begun to understand why Chris was so passionate when he said that even though he must serve under every President and party, it really matters who runs our country. He might not have been willing to admit when he needed a map at Mount Sinai, but he was right about a lot of crucially important things.

Because of Chris, I expect more from our politicians now than I did before his death led me on this quest. Why should we give politicians a pass when they fail to carry out their mission? Shouldn't they be held to the same standard that Chris Stevens applied to himself?

At one time I might have been willing to give Hillary Clinton the benefit of the doubt, but no longer. Hillary Clinton's choice to sit still, leaving Americans alone, entirely on their own, to fend for themselves in Benghazi, will go down in history as a singular act of cowardice unmatched by anyone who desires to win the position of the Presidency. The choice was Secretary Clinton's to make, to either scrap the mission or improve the security. But you do not desert your countrymen who it is your duty to protect, leaving your most important asset in a meat grinder to die.

AUTHOR'S NOTE

I feel a deep sorrow for the grief Chris's mother, Mary Commanday has had to endure. The loss of a child is pain that is beyond the understanding of anyone who has never felt its sharp agony. However, despite her wishes that Chris's name not be politicized, there is sadly, nothing she can do about this. The political campaigning process is about issues that affect the candidate's suitability to lead the country and Benghazi is very pertinent. Trump is not to everyone's liking but he did get the Republican nomination and he is running for President against Clinton. As such, he is entitled legally to use any facts that he deems crucial to showing his adversary's flaws.

There was an entire inquiry held to investigate Chris's murder and Hillary Clinton's culpability in that tragedy. His death was totally preventable and the bottom line is that he shouldn't be dead, nor should Sean Smith, Tyrone Woods or Glen Doherty. No one has dibs on who can or cannot speak of Benghazi or Chris. As he will forever be linked with the others who perished there, you cannot separate him from them. To do so would be to silence and violate the rights of their family members to question the circumstances surrounding the deaths of their loved ones, as in the case of Patricia Smith, Sean's mother and Charles Woods, Tyrone Woods' father.

In a democratic society, all citizens, not just a select few, have a right to express their opinions and to discuss what will and has already become a historic event and a legacy of the Obama administration. To understand what happened and to uncover the truth, we must be able to have a free discussion about everything and everyone connected to the horrific events of September 11, 2012 in Benghazi Libya.

Some of the proceeds from the sale of this book are being donated to WIRED International, a nonprofit, volunteer-driven organization that has been delivering medical and health education to conflict-affected and underserved regions since 1997. In October 2015, WIRED International launched a community health education initiative honoring the late Ambassador J. Christopher Stevens. Since Ambassador Chris Stevens believed in community engagement and public diplomacy, his philosophy corresponds with WIRED's longstanding approach to programs and practices. WIRED's extensive health education programs in Iraq and in Jordan provide useful and relevant experience in reaching medical professionals and grassroots populations in the Middle East. The present initiative will extend globally and will reach out to countries throughout the Middle East, including Libya.

Chris Stevens has changed me. He changed me when I met him, loved him, lost him. He changed me even more when he made me grieve for him so much that I embarked on the journey that I just told you about. At the core of my journey was Chris Stevens, for without his magnificent character and qualities, there would have been no journey worth the name and no standard against which to evaluate the conduct of those connected to his death.

Chris's murder in Benghazi on September 11th 2012, collapsed time for me, as though everything I had done with him and felt for him had just occurred yesterday. All of my memories of our time together—even the painful times—were suddenly cast in glorious light. Only the good times stood out. Yet I knew that my memory was playing tricks.

Equally important, I could not let my new love Michael compete with this image of my time with Chris. There is an unwritten rule among couples that love each other: never discuss first loves because current loves never measure up to the lies our hearts tell us about that special memory that only the first can leave behind. This is why I had never told Michael who Chris was until the day of the news report of his death.

ABOUT THE AUTHOR

Lydie M. Denier is an accomplished actress, demonstrating her versatility with appearances in over forty television series and feature films. She is best known as Yasmine Bernoudi on General Hospital, Jane on Tarzan, the television series, and Nicole on the series Acapulco Heat. On stage, she portrayed the title role of the iconic movie star Greta Garbo.

Lydie has traveled far from the countryside in France where she grew up watching old American movies on television while dreaming of becoming an actress. Her journeys have taken her to exotic lands and her experiences have been diverse. Now, as she enters this next stage of her life as more of a writer than an actress, she embraces it with all the joie de vivre for which the French are famous.

Lydie currently lives in beautiful Laguna Beach, California, where, as an excellent chef, she loves to cook when she is not writing or acting.

Photo Credits: Lydie M Denier's private collection and U.S. State Department.

LydieMDenier@gmail.com
www.LydieMDenier.com

Made in the USA
San Bernardino, CA
09 February 2017